Sometimes There's a Hole in the Ceiling

Sometimes There's a Hole in the Ceiling

Barry L. Johnson

Abingdon
Nashville and New York

SOMETIMES THERE'S A HOLE IN THE CEILING

Copyright © 1975 by Abingdon

Library of Congress Cataloging in Publication Data

JOHNSON, BARRY LEE, 1943-   Sometimes there's a hole in
the ceiling. Includes bibliographical references. 1. Christian
life—Methodist authors. I. Title.
BV4501.2.J53   248'.48'7   74-30431

ISBN 0-687-39084-2

Scripture quotations noted RSV are from the Revised Standard Version of the Bible, copyrighted 1946, 1952, and 1971
by the Division of Christian Education, National Council of
Churches, and are used by permission.

"Songs in the Night," letter from Richard and Lean Acosta
with Heidi and Markie, in *Soundings*, edited by Robert A.
Raines, is copyright © 1970 by Robert A. Raines, and is
reprinted by permission of Harper & Row, Publishers, Inc.

MANUFACTURED BY THE PARTHENON PRESS AT
NASHVILLE, TENNESSEE, UNITED STATES OF AMERICA

To Mary
The most gracious hole-knocker of all
And to
James R. and Elizabeth Johnson
Who first taught me to look

Preface

As an eight-year-old kid I made my first commitment to Jesus Christ. Now, I am not certain whether that promise was prompted by a personal need or the knowledge that it would make my mother's day to see it happen. Initial motivation notwithstanding, I have never forsaken that commitment. Through a pre-teen bout with rheumatic fever, a high school career as a would-be athlete and a recognized speech champion, a passive sojourn at a conservative college, three years of academic discovery in seminary, six years of local parish experience, and three thrilling years as executive director for EURISKON, I have hungered after the will of God. Often, personal attitudes and actions shroud that commitment. But when masks are removed, images pushed to the side, and rebelliousness stifled, I find myself yearning to know what Christ would have me be for him. Rarely am I certain—but always I am searching.

If you are fully satisfied with your faith the way it is, stop now—don't read this book. However, if, like me, you know the gnawing vacuum that comes when you have given yourself time and again to Christ yet are still thirsting after further knowledge of him, read on—you may find some light. If you like simple formulas and chains of command that relieve you of the burden of growth, stop now. But if you can accept total freedom, responsibly, read on. If yours is a faith without doubt, stop now. But if from time to time you must ask yourself, "Is Christianity worth a damn?" read on.

This book will not leave you with a sense of smug self-righteousness. If you're looking for somebody to say you've been right all along, you have the wrong source. I hope it will leave you with a humble warmth that whispers, "Lead on, O King eternal, the day of march has come."

Sometimes There's a Hole in the Ceiling is written for the person who has played out all the options; for the average Christian who aches for a fresh experience with Christ; for the thinker who has reasoned himself to the point of inanity; for the ordinary guy who feels terribly cheated when others bubble about marvelous experiences with Christ; for the middleperson who likes to feel the faith but not gush it. It is a theological statement, an unanswered question, and a chronological study all rolled into a systematic investigation of growth-oriented Christianity. But, most of all, it is an echo of Isaiah's promise: "They that wait upon the Lord shall renew their strength; they shall mount up with wings as eagles; they shall run, and not be weary; and they shall walk, and not faint." That's where I am. That's why I write.

Barry Johnson
1975

Contents

Introduction
The Search   11

Chapter One
The Light in Man   17

Chapter Two
The Light in Circumstance   28

Chapter Three
The Light in Hope   37

Chapter Four
The Light in Freedom   46

Chapter Five
The Light in Forgiveness   56

Chapter Six
The Light in Growth   65

Chapter Seven
The Light in Community   76

Chapter Eight
The Light in Selfhood   87

Chapter Nine
The Light in Love   100

Chapter Ten
The Light in the Word   111

Appendix
Small Group Discussion Questions   121

Notes   125

Introduction

The Search

Fred Norman reluctantly reached for the off-on switch on his bedside TV. His wife had been sleeping since Johnny Carson's monologue was half over. "Moments to Live By" was on now. Fred was still tense from a tough day in the office; he couldn't stomach the multisyllabic babbling of the preacher before him. He hit the switch and lay in the silent darkness, brooding. God? Five hundred sermons, thirteen years of church school, and thousands of awkward prayers ago, he had heard that title for the first time. Now, it seemed as unreal as if he had never heard it before. The search would continue.

The 6:11 was due in three minutes. Wilma Edson stared through the rain-dotted windshield. Supper was on, the kids were watching "Sesame Street," and Ted would soon appear. Suit wrinkled, tie agape, the evening paper in his hand, he would slide into the seat, kiss her while changing the radio station, and they would go home. This is the abundant life? She was searching too.

The stiff confirmation robe made him sit taller. Still, Bernie Miller didn't feel right about the whole thing. For two years, sixty miserable Saturdays, he had endured the process. Now, thoroughly programmed about the nature of God, he was ready to join the church and take his place in the Kingdom. He looked at the worshipers. Maude Ellis was gazing out the window. Uncle Ralph was meditating, both eyes shut. John Raines was playing hangman with Herbie Green. Mrs. McAdoo, the preachers' wife, had her head in its tilted "in church" position. And his father, Jack Miller, was glaring right back at him. Apparently he wasn't supposed to be looking. But he was, and in his heart he knew he would continue to do so. He was yet to discover a God who was real.

Few of us have difficulty relating to the feelings these people were experiencing. The search for God is an endless and, for many, hopeless task. There are some who learn to cope with it, but most develop a method of answerless acceptance. Our seminaries are filled with searchers, men and women who come to educate their way to God. Many leave as hungry as when they arrived. Some choose other fields of endeavor; others continue their search as pastors. To develop a complex awareness of the presence of God in a day of overcrowded schedules is a universal Christian concern.

Some center their search in the church. No job is turned down, no committee overlooked. Every task brings a new dream that the fullness of God's presence just might be realized in toiling for the temple. Serving tea for the Naomi Circle, flipping pancakes for the Easter breakfast, rolling cancer bandages, fixing the parsonage sump pump, or fretting through a council meeting— somewhere, somehow, someday, they tell themselves, God has to emerge.

Milt Evans was like that. (I am certain the addition to his home was prompted by the need for hat storage space.) He never mastered the word "no." When his wife was seriously ill, I couldn't bring myself to look into his tired eyes as he catechized, "Barry, a God of love wouldn't do this, would he?" He had dumped his life into the church. He still wasn't sure. Thousands can echo his sentiments. Their lives are the fuel with which the church continues to move. But is God any more real? Is the search satisfactorily culminated? Is the vision more crystallized?

Often those searching most painstakingly are the most outwardly confident—so much so that they are avoided because of their ardor. They pass out tracts, quote the Scriptures, amass conversion scalps, despise sin, and cry themselves to sleep. They know how hungry they are. If bearing a cross is the secret, these poor souls ought to be sleeping in God's arms. But, repeatedly, the strictness of their life-style only betrays their lack of closeness to a God who loves them as they are.

I was beset by one of these people while working in a little hamlet in upstate New York. She was fortyish and her purse was bursting with tracts. Two adolescent boys bounced in her wake. "Do you know the Holy Spirit?" she inquired. The fire in her eyes and the set of her jaw betrayed the depth of her commitment. "I think so," I answered. She started to bubble. "Isn't it great? I've had him for several years and I've brought many others. It took every day after school for a month to get my oldest boy . . . but it finally happened. He burst forth in the most fantastic tongue. Too bad these people can't get there, heh?" As she walked away the elder brother slipped me an elbow. Looking at him, I was relieved. He didn't say a word, just winked. That said it. He was helping in her search, and she didn't even know how he really felt.

George Robbins is a student at a small college in Ohio. In keeping with the trend of the last few years, there is an ardent group of Jesus people on the campus. One evening George was coerced into attending their weekly meeting. His account of what happened evokes laughter, tears, and a good deal of concern. The first thirty minutes covered testimonies regarding the events of the week. George tried to share some of his own anxieties, but was restrained by a friend who knew he "wasn't a real Christian." Next came the real trial. The leader prayed that someone would speak in tongues, and forty-five minutes of silence set in. The group broke into applause when George began to mumble. Seizing him by the hand, the leader demanded eagerly, "George, are you speaking in tongues?" George's answer is food for thought in a time of searching: "Heck no, I'm talking to myself. Nobody else would listen."

The search for God is not limited to the laity. Frequently those most haunted by it are ministers. Week after week they piece their struggle together. Careful not to tip their hand, yet longing for support, they are forced by the pastoral image to measure their candor. What a relief it would be to step up before the congregation and ask, "Where are you, Lord? Where are you?"

A rare venture into the South confirmed my belief that even the best have questions. Sitting on the screened porch of one of the finest preachers in Tennessee, I was amazed to hear him express his doubt: "What is the church? What is ministry? What is the Kingdom of God? What is God?" This guy held a prestigious pulpit at an early stage of his ministry. Counseling, planning, preaching, or singing, he was first-class. But apparently all the glamour of his much-coveted position didn't satisfy his need. At this point, he was no longer a counselor, preacher, or musician: he was just a man in search of his Maker.

This book is the work of a fellow searcher. Listening to others questioning the presence of God, I have wanted to offer simple, much-turned clichés in response. But all the time I am aware that the moment of doubt is as much mine as it is theirs. That is what prompted my writing. Not that I have captured a formula. I have not. Rather, I have decided that the search can never be absolutely concluded. Our inability to confine and define the presence of God is but a measure of the challenge to us as his children. The key to peaceful searching lies in commitment and in training our sensors to be receptive. All of us have them. We simply have not learned how to make them work to our advantage. Every day, every hour, every moment brings the fresh hope of further revelation. The question remains: Are we open enough to sense the presence of a God of love who never loses contact with our lives?

My search was accented during my junior year at Wheaton College, when the short-story professor wrote a title on the board and instructed us to write a story to fit it. The title was "Sometimes There's a Hole in the Ceiling." After much effort, many crumpled pages, and unsolicited coaching from my housebrothers, I whipped up a story about a ghetto family that received unexpected help from an unexpected source. The story closed with "Sometimes there's a hole in the ceiling; it was made for the hand of God." When the paper came back with an A minus, the whole house celebrated the victory. I have wondered since whether the grade was prompted by quality or content. I hope it was both.

Some years have passed since that paper was written. Once, wanting to see it again, I spent an entire evening rummaging through my old college and seminary papers. Alas, it was not to be found. It's just as well. The paper was an experience, and experiences are nearly impossible to repeat. Since I wrote it, my mind has been challenged by real live seminary professors and long-dead theologians; I have felt the ups and downs of a suburban ministry; and a wife and two children have replaced the house-brothers. The hole in the ceiling has grown. I am still searching, and I suppose I always will be; but I am also increasingly aware that the presence of God is limited only by our perception.

Chapter One

The Light in Man

Winter in Chicago means wind; bitter, sharp, harsh, unrelenting wind. Nowhere is that wind more pitiless than on West Madison Street. Here the derelicts of the city wrap themselves in cardboard and huddle in alleys to avoid the wind's icy wrath. As a college student I used to drive my friends through that area just to watch their faces as they witnessed the hopelessness that marks Skid Row. Now I had a new purpose. I was doing a three-session program for the Chicago Christian Industrial League, a self-help agency specializing in vocational rehabilitation.

I made it a point to arrive early each evening. The atmosphere didn't appeal to me, but I felt I had to relate to the men if I was going to grow with them. Furthermore, parking places were easier to find in the daylight. As I made my way past the cheap wine stores to the chapel, a raggedy, stooped little man with an impeccable goatee stopped me. He wanted some change for a cup of coffee. The lines of pain were already etched on his face—he was no newcomer to Madison Street—but when I said, "No," a fresh hurt showed in his eyes. I had noticed him at the meeting the night before, and I am sure he was confident that I would help him. After all, I talked such a good game; how could I say no? But I did. As he turned to shuffle off I saw in him legions of men who have heard the Good News but never felt it. We are so great at telling people how to find God; why are we so slow at touching their hands, meeting them at their point of need, and leading them to him? Why do we talk so big and carry such a small stick? It's hard to worry about your soul when your lips are cracked and your belly is growling. My thoughts collected, I raised my hand to beckon him. But it was too late; he was gone.

I had a job to do. I went in and started to preach a great sermon. Right. I didn't believe a word of it. I kept seeing that quaint face with hope all over it crumbling to pieces when I said no. Then he came in. There was no fanfare, just the scraping of the chair amidst the coughing of the men. As he nodded to me a ray of light burst through my ceiling. Though I had said no to him, it was his choice to say yes to me. He didn't have to be there. The CCIL doesn't demand chapel participation of those who want a bed. He was there because he wanted to be.

Acceptance in the face of rejection stands at the heart of practical Christianity, and it always happens through people. Through people, the presence of God is crystallized.

I suppose this is the meaning of the Incarnation. God became man in order to accept man. John puts it this way: "The Word became flesh and dwelt among us" (1:14 RSV). I like that. The phrase just rolls out. It's even more meaningful when we note the history of the term translated as "dwelt." It means "pitched his tent." Think of the weight of that term to the nomadic tribesmen of Christ's day. To them, a tent was everything: a place to sleep, a place to eat, a place to make love, a place to bear children, a place to *be*. To say, "God pitched his tent with us" is to indelibly record the fact that God speaks through man.

When that street dweller slipped into the chapel on Skid Row, he pitched his tent with me. He met me on my terms. He was waiting for me again on the last night. He found me in the back room where I usually left my coat and briefcase. As soon as I saw him, I started to dig for a quarter. He stopped me.

"No, man, its OK," he blurted out. "I just wanted you to know I'm going home."

"Great!" I responded. "Who's going to meet you?"

"I don't know. I haven't been there for fifteen years."

As I stood speechless, he shook my hand and left. The door closed behind him, and I realized anew that God uses us most when we manipulate least.

The ability to spot the presence of God in those around us is not automatic. It demands cultivation. It calls for moments of pondering when we sift through an event, encounter, or personality and consciously dig for evidence of the love of God. Sometimes it shows in an overlooked phrase, a facial expression, a specific act, something left unsaid, or even a rebuke. Still, I am convinced, if we look close enough it can always be found. The trick is to limit our preconceptions.

This truth was placed vividly before me when we were concluding a program in Northern Illinois. The evidence of the experience sits in my office today. I was standing with the pastor as the participants were leaving. There were some small groups still standing around talking, but the program was over and I was beginning to relax. A tug at my coat made me look down. A little boy (he couldn't have been more than four years old) was standing in front of me with his hands cupped.

"I got somethin' for ya," he stammered shyly.

Assuming that he had money, I was embarrassed. "That's OK, tiger," I said. "You keep your money."

"Wait a minute, jerky," the pastor interrupted (we knew each other well). "He brought it for you—take it."

One glance at the little fella's face told me my friend was right. I put out my hand and in one movement the boy dropped something in it and turned away. I watched him scoot across the room to his mother. When I looked at the gift, my heart melted. There, in my hand, was a tiny, purple hot-wheels car. It is one of the most precious things I have ever received. Why? because it is a part of that little kid, that's why. I am certain that car was more valuable to that child than any amount of money. Gazing at it, I see hours of living room carpet races, and miles of sandbox adventures. When he gave it to me, he pitched his tent next to mine. He gave me a corner of his life, and it made him a lifelong friend—even if I never see him again.

In this regard, children are masters at knocking holes in ceilings. William Schutz captures the feeling when he writes of the impact on his life of his infant son.

And his pleasure now, during his first fifteen months, is mainly physical—being thrown up in the air, sliding off the refrigerator, into his father's arms, being tickled and hugged, having his cheeks chewed, his behind munched, having his face caressed, rubbing his cheek against another's cheek. And he touches. It's hard to match the feeling of his little fingers exploring my teeth way inside my mouth while his face has that curious, intent look.

And on it goes. He is joyful and he gives joy. He wakes up each morning eager for new adventure. Maybe today it will be a piece of string, or the toilet plunger, or the telephone, or pots and pans, or—more rarely—a new toy.

Ethan is joy. He enjoys each aspect of his life with his whole being. He gives joy to those near him. His joy is contagious.[1]

Perhaps this instance of awareness is even more authentic than the others I have mentioned. Motivation can

be questioned in the other cases, but not in the spontaneous actions of a fifteen-month-old child. All he was doing
was pitching his tent with his father, living with him,
sharing his existence.

Pete Adams, an eastern associate of mine, picks up the
same theme when he tells about his second son. The first
boy was a natural jock, but not the second. Whereas the
older boy was husky and competitive, his brother was
slight and passive. Therefore, when the younger lad decided to play Little League football, his dad was thrilled.
To show his support, Pete agreed to man the yard mar-
kers. It was a long season. They lost their first five games,
and although he was the starting quarterback it was obvious that Teddy would never match the record of his elder
brother. The sixth game brought a moment of truth. At
half time there was no score. The glimmer of hope grew
brighter when in the third quarter, through a steady rain,
Teddy's team slogged to the opponents' two-yard line.
Two line plunges and an off-tackle slant made it fourth
and goal from one foot. Pete said he could see the strain
stamped on Teddy's face as they broke the huddle.

"Set, hut, 29, 32, hut, hut!"

It was a quarterback sneak, and Teddy bounced six
inches into the end zone. Daddy's heart jumped into his
throat. His mud-splattered kid leaped in the air and
threw the ball triumphantly to the ground. Then he deliberately turned to face his father. The joy of the moment had already made Pete's eyes brim. Now he saw the
tears making ruddy paths down Teddy's cheeks. As the
father explains, "When our eyes met, I knew that our
tears were for each other. They went on to lose the game,
but it really didn't matter. We had found common
ground."

As we struggle to comprehend the hole in the ceiling,

we must make deliberate efforts to find common ground with each person who crosses our path. When we succeed, a new wholeness fills our lives.

I found a helping of this wholeness while attending a convention in San Francisco. I was sharing a room with Bill Johnson, former chairman of the Board of Evangelism for the Northern Illinois Conference of The United Methodist Church. It was about two in the morning and both of us were still awake. We had been touring the city of the Golden Gate and it took some time to unwind. As we chatted, Bill began to muse. His thoughts, I have since discovered, are not uncommon for veteran preachers.

"Barry, I'm not sure . . . about my ministry, I mean. Here I am, forty-three years old, and I've only got a church of six hundred members. You know I'm not the smartest guy in the world. . . ."

I didn't hear the rest of what he said. I didn't want to. We had long since found our common ground, for it was Bill Johnson, more than anyone else, who helped nail my dream together. As a rookie I had no idea how to fly a new program. He gave me wings.

My first Board of Evangelism meeting is a typical example. The board was outlining its programs for the coming year and had come to an impasse. On one side sat the conservatives, screaming for some "real evangelism." On the other sat the social concern people, babbling in foot-long terms about evangelism involving the total work of the church. With the EURISKON outlines in my brief-case it was all I could do to keep quiet (though I was terrified at the possibility of rejection). Two hours into the meeting we had gotten nowhere. Then Bill Johnson looked at me and opened a door: "You're new on the board. What do you think?" Forty-five minutes later the board had a new pilot project called EURISKON—and I had found a wise counselor who cared about my dream and had made a life-style of opening doors.

Bill is a people-builder. His parish extends far beyond the boundaries of his church. As the pioneer of the prison-release ministry in Illinois, he has touched hundreds of lives at the point of hurt. Job hunting, clothes buying, sharing a story, or as the affirming end of a therapeutic phone call, Bill gets things done. Bishop Thomas Pryor echoed my sentiments when he said, "Bill Johnson is one of those rare people who can find something good in anybody."

In the months that followed that first meeting Bill became a major hole-knocker in my life. Of necessity, I had to work my way through the maze of political connections that make up The United Methodist Church. At every turn, skepticism, sometimes downright cynicism, abounded. The fundamentalists thought the program was too radical. The liberals put it down as "Billy Graham evangelism." Both groups fell victim to the combined influence of ignorance and deep-seated fears. The conservatives knew only what they wanted, the liberals only what they didn't want. I was caught in the middle. Through it all, Bill was there. He nursed the pilot project through the program council. He battled with the treasurer for promotional funds. He took every opportunity to introduce me to new people. And when the time came for me to step out of the local parish, he cooperated with the bishop and his cabinet to set me free for twenty-six weeks of the year.

Now, in San Francisco, listening to him questioning his ministry was too much for me. I don't know why, but I didn't even speak. I simply made up my mind to affirm the guy every chance I got.

God speaks through men. Where else do we experience acceptance in spite of our failures? Where else can attitudes challenge us to grow? Where else do we find a sustaining measure of love by which to gauge our worth? Our vexation comes as we inventory our relationships and sense our blindness.

Every Don Quixote needs a Sancho Panza. Marty Mogk is mine. From the day the Mogk family entered the church ours has been a friendship anchored in love. During the embryonic stage of EURISKON's growth, Marty would drive a forklift for eight hours then jump in his car and drive eighty or ninety miles to give me moral support at a program site. Often he wouldn't get home until three or four in the morning. His workday started at seven, but that didn't seem to matter: he'd be back again the next night. On one occasion he drove back two hundred miles to get my preaching stool while I forged on to another church.

The ultimate affirmation offered by Marty came on a cold December night in 1971. By then I was secretary of our Board of Evangelism and, on this particular evening, was to chair a meeting in the suburb of Elmhurst. I was twenty minutes late and my head was jammed. I had already decided to give up the security of my pastoral appointment and plunge full-time into EURISKON. D day was to be January 1, 1972. The pressure was massive—particularly with only a thousand dollars in the bank. Preoccupied with all these thoughts, I didn't even notice Marty's car as I pulled into the parking lot. Charging for the door, late for the meeting and bugged about the future, I was shocked when Marty blocked my path.

Holding up a white envelope, he announced, "Betty and I want you to have this." His firm German face underlined what I already knew: he was too stubborn to take no for an answer. Furthermore, I really had to get to the meeting. I said, "Thanks, brother," took the envelope, and went into the church, figuring they had scraped up forty or fifty dollars and wanted to encourage me. My mistake was waiting until I was standing before the Board of Evangelism to open the envelope. They looked so bewildered when I couldn't talk. In my hand were five crisp hundred-dollar bills.

Marty Mogk has a family of six and an uncle who shares his roof. At that time he was making heavy house payments and driving a used Dodge to work. The only way he could have come up with five hundred dollars was to borrow it. In so doing he told me he believed in me even more than I did. His wholeness illumined mine. He pitched his tent with me, and the hole in the ceiling spilled new light.

There have been others: many who said, "You can do it," and made me believe it; a Rockford businessman who paid my secretary for the first twenty-two weeks; a golfing parishioner who sweetened the kitty at just the right time; a willing and brave brother-in-law who let me test the program in his church; children who painstakingly scratched out letters of appreciation; scores who gave three dollars a month to get us started; and of course, a wife who shared the common waves of an adventure that knows no end.

She was there when it started at my brother-in-law's church in Connecticut, and her participation was twofold: in the program itself and in my joy over its success. I can still see the glorious New England countryside whipping past the car as we drove away and I explained, "Honey, I can't sit on it. It means hitting the road—but I've got to chase my dream." There wasn't even a pause. She slipped across the seat, clutched my hand, smiled, and said, "Do it." Through four years of money pressures, lonesome nights, and many decisions she has had to make alone, her attitude has not changed.

It hasn't been easy for her. Tracy was five months old when the program started, and Dane was born ten months later. Couple the scramble of two in diapers with the calamity of a husband whose head is locked into changing the negative image of evangelism in the main-line church, and you sense the challenge that she faced. Still, I didn't even realize the pressure on her until one summer evening when I opened a kitchen cabinet and found a message she had pinned to greet herself every time she reached for another glass for the kids: "Every morning: Be of good courage. Every evening: Well done." When I saw it, my gut tightened. My selfishness was never more painful. This time it was the grace of a silent partner that smashed a new hole in the ceiling.

But what does all this mean to those who aren't building a national evangelical program? What does it mean to a harried engineer, a bartender, or a mother who doubles as a checker at the supermarket? How does it fit in a farmhouse, a suburban tri-level, or a ghetto rattrap?

It fits in every situation where personal relationships are possible. Obviously, that means everywhere. The challenge to knock fresh holes in the ceiling is multiplied every time person meets person. And it is not limited to new relationships.

In response to that challenge, each of us can further our awareness of God's presence by reassessing our relationships to the members of our own family. In fact, these relationships are invariably the best hole-knockers. They are based on a fuller perspective. The good and the bad find balance in sustained acquaintance. Different kinds of smiles, voice tone, body posture, and eye contact add new

26

overtones when people really know each other. It's a matter of awareness, and when we understand that God speaks through man we realize that such an awareness must be three-dimensional. No longer do we feel things simply as individuals. Now there is a new "we" that encompasses the sensor, the sensed, and the source of sensing (God himself). My wife becomes a woman, my woman, God's woman, and the kids' woman all at the same time. When I can keep in focus all those demands on her person, she also becomes a hole-knocker, a vessel of God's love.

That kind of reasoning can be applied anywhere. The only prerequisite is accepting the uniqueness of every person—bartender, engineer, housewife, check-out girl, jockey, preacher, prostitute, and pimp—as a child of God. To live that truth is to recognize the first hole in your ceiling.

Chapter Two

The Light in Circumstance

It was a foggy winter afternoon, and I was driving through central Illinois on Route 66, better known as Interstate 55. I had the automatic speed control engaged and was doing some brain churning. Often my most inspired thoughts surface while I am driving alone. Route 66 is a divided four-lane road. In the last ten years I have become thoroughly familiar with it as I have frequently trekked homeward to see my parents. In other words, it had become a boring ride. Never again. I was moving at about seventy miles an hour when I noticed a huge gush of smoke and dust from beneath a truck across the median. The next thing I saw was a massive black object hurtling right at my windshield. I didn't even have time to hit the brakes. I felt my naval perched on the end of my tongue. Fortunately, the timing was just right and all I received was a fleeting glimpse of a ten-inch section of truck tire. I slowed down.

Had I been moving two miles an hour faster, had the trucker paused to blow his nose before leaving the last truck stop, that chunk of tire would have smashed my windshield, and possibly killed me. But I wasn't and he didn't—and life goes on, and the hole in the ceiling gets a little bigger.

Most of us can think of similar close shaves we have had. But how many of us are willing to accept the fact that God works through circumstance? How many of us have a mature enough faith to believe "for everything there is a season, and a time for every matter under heaven" (Ecclesiastes 3:1 RSV). However, as the patchwork incidents of life blend together into the unique experience of each person, one is forced to recognize God's hand at work.

Ultimately, we are talking about control and the lack of it. As long as we think we can completely control our own destiny, most of us feel we have no need for a God of love. Perhaps this is why simplistic, overcontrolling systems of faith are so popular right now. But at the moment when we lose control, the idea of an omnipotent being who cares about *me* as an individual in spite of myself becomes comfortingly pleasant.

When we stop trying to manipulate everything that happens to us and freely give ourselves to the unfolding of God's will, his love shows itself in circumstance. God speaks to us all the time; we just have to shut up, and listen, and look, and let go.

God works through circumstance—the good, the bad, and the unexpected. Ours is but to accept what he gives and wait. "For everything there is a season, and a time for every matter under heaven."

Remember the Zacchaeus incident in the nineteenth chapter of Luke. So often, when we deal with it, we concentrate on the roles of the characters: Zacchaeus as a rich yet penitent sinner, Christ as the agent of grace. This time let's forget those facts and deal with circumstance. To begin with, Zacchaeus was curious. He wanted to see the commotion-creating preacher. Secondly, Zacchaeus was a runt. When he reached the place where the Lord was, he couldn't even see over the crowd. Now, let's stop the story right there and consider what might have happened.

As one who despises waiting for anything, I am quick to react to the tax collector's predicament. It's like going to the theatre and discovering a line two blocks long. When that happens, I don't go to the show. Had Zacchaeus been blessed with my disposition the story would have been over. But he wasn't. He was inventive. When one avenue of progress was blocked, he soon found another. Sure, it was an inconvenience. And he must have looked a fool climbing that tree. But he did it. And because he did it, Christ was able to relate to him in a positive manner, to the advantage of Zacchaeus and everybody who saw the exchange.

Zacchaeus was stymied. He could have quit. But because he didn't, the hole in the ceiling brought forth new knowledge of the love of God. The unfolding of circumstance coupled with one man's determined reaction yielded the Good News in vital, existential, tangible terms.

By the time I reached the final semester of my seminary career I had learned to love the life-style of the student. The warmth and security of academic endeavor in the personal setting of the seminary was as real to me as the womb of a mother to a baby. In a certain sense, it was also as protective. I certainly wasn't coming in contact with the sweat, pressure, and pickiness of the world around me. It's much more comfortable to dream about loving, sacrificial service than it is to live it. Thus, when a professor mentioned the possibility of continuing my education and getting a doctorate, I was mesmerized by the whole idea. Dr. Barry Johnson—that lit my fuse. First I located a seminary that offered the degree I wanted (theology and preaching). Then I began the systematic process of filling out forms, completing applications, and carefully selecting the right persons to write my recommendations. Finally there were two examinations I needed to take. One was a graduate-work qualification test administered by a local university. I took it. The other was the Minnesota Multiphasic Psychological Exam. The institution to which I was applying mailed the test to one of my professor friends, who was to supervise as I wrote it. However, that particular professor was not at all fond of watching students choose A, B, C, or none of the above, so he just handed it to me with instructions to bring it in when I was finished. I thought that was great. I went directly to the library, rolled up my sleeves, and started to "stack" that test. As unfamiliar terms popped up, I proceeded to track down definitions. When obviously loaded psychological references surfaced, readily available psychological textbooks helped me understand how to answer. I even found an analysis of the Minnesota Multiphasic to work with. And when certain questions were repeated I developed a system whereby I always answered the same way. After all, aren't doctors of theology supposed to be consistent? It took six hours to take the test, review it and adjust it to perfection.

Six weeks after I returned that test to the professor I had still not heard a word about my acceptance. I wasn't worried. I even went to my district superintendent and secured a list of part-time appointments that might dovetail with my academic development.

When it got to be ten weeks, I began to stew. I sat down and wrote a personal letter to the admissions director. Within the week, I received my answer. It came in one of those sterile, short, block-style letters. I didn't have to read it; I knew what it said. For the record, it alluded to the undersupply of teachers and the oversupply of students. The point was simple: I didn't make it. After the letter came, I sat in our apartment for two hours. I didn't eat. I didn't write. I didn't read. I didn't move. I just sat.

31

Today, the hurt has diminished. The value I set on a doctorate has decreased—although I'd still like to have one someday. And, more important, EURISKON could never have developed in a seminary setting. The funny thing is, years afterward I still didn't believe the oversupply-undersupply bit, so I questioned a dear friend who had followed up on the application. His reply is the crowning touch: "They said everything was great except your psychological. It was a mass of confusion!"

When we must keep control, when we try to determine our own destiny, when we seek to con the Creator—we lose every time. Circumstance may well be the greatest communications line ever created between God and man.

The recognition of affirmative circumstance is pivotal as we seek to live a life-style consistent with our faith. Of necessity there will always be those moments when we take a "leap of faith." Sometimes we are successful; other times it's catastrophic. The trick is to learn from both. Failure demands careful analysis of motivation and procedure. Success calls for an understanding of the real power source that makes things happen. There is no such thing as a self-made man. Apart from the grace of God we wouldn't even have life, let alone the abundance that so many of us have found.

Three months after leaving the local pastorate I became very restless. As I looked at the months ahead I could see disaster approaching. We had a complete schedule until the end of May, but the summer brought visions of Humphrey Bogart dying in the desert. There was one program in June, none in July, and one in August. Two options were obvious: (1) cut expenses; (2) find more work. The first wouldn't be difficult. I won't spend what I don't have. There goes the office, the secretary, and the mimeo machine. As a kid I had learned to letter signs while hanging around my dad's sign shop. I wasn't great, but I was good enough to put names on pickup trucks. I thought of a summer sitting on Coke cases using a number eight quill and guessing at empty weights. Not very glorious—but it would keep food on the table. Creating more work certainly had more appeal. The master manipulator began to scheme.

I was not to work alone. Don Sanberg is an advertising consultant. He is also a first-class dreamer. Shortly after discovering the need for summer work, I was having lunch with Don and shared my concern. I could see his wheels starting to turn. By the time the lunch was over we had planned a magnificent event to save the summer. We called the thing Serendipity '72. It consisted of a family weekend at a Chicago hotel complete with seminars on the fruits of the Spirit. On paper, it had the potential not only to save the summer but to fill the kitty for six months thereafter. It proved to be one of the most monumental mistakes I have ever made. As I write this, we are still paying for our folly.

I should have known it was a flop when Sanberg and I had to drive through a blinding snowstorm to get to the hotel to set things up. But alas, my vision was separated from reality by my egocentric conviction that it was a deal no one could turn down. Sanberg designed a beautiful three-color brochure; I found a printer who would carry us until the cash started to flow; and we frantically began to develop our mailing list.

A fabulous weekend in Chicago spiced with a poolside luau and the spiritual insights of guru Johnson—who could turn it down? Five hundred dollars in mailing, one thousand in printing, and five weeks of cold sweat gave us our answer: everybody could. It was too expensive. Chicago wasn't that appealing, and neither was I. We received four reservations. Eating crow is writing four letters to explain how ineffective money motivation can be. Serendipity '72 bombed. The hardest part of all was calling an old high school sweetheart who had accepted the invitation and telling her that ol' cool Barry didn't have it together after all. The summer was at hand and I was searching for a Coke case.

On May 15 I paid the last of our bills; there was $156 left in the bank and no programs until June 15. I prayed for some vision. In my eyes, the hole in the ceiling was shrinking fast.

When pressure is high, there are two directions in which I move. First, I maroon myself and make peace with reality. I decided that if God wanted me to paint pickup trucks, that's what I would do. Secondly, I find a friend and share my worries. This time my friend was an old seminary acquaintance in Ohio. Terry Litton is a brooder. He's a specialist at tackling the impossible. I think he actually gets a kick out of it. Sitting at his kitchen table I spilled out my anxiety about the summer. It was a relief just to see someone else furrow a brow in my behalf. He didn't stop there. He gave me a "maybe" address. (A "maybe" address is the name of a person who can help—*maybe*.) Then he set it up so I could meet the lady in question. I have never been big on begging. I don't like to be begged from and I don't like to beg from someone else. This is one of the glories of God's grace: it's not to be begged, it's to be accepted. Thus, after meeting the gracious lady, I decided to write a forthright letter to her explaining my goals, outlining my progress, and identifying my predicament. The *maybe* became a *yes!* No reasons. No pressure. No manipulation. Just a beautiful Christian person granting support to a heartfelt cause. Over the **next thirty months this woman gave over fifty thousand** dollars to my ministry. A steady rain fell through the hole in the ceiling, bringing new life to the parched earth at my feet. EURISKON had found its affirmation.

God works through circumstance. He gives us motivation, opportunity, and ability. We must never seek to control any of those gifts. As he sees fit, our needs will be met. When we expose our sensors we will feel his presence. Centuries have passed since Paul wrote, in Galatians 4:4, "When the fulness of the time was come, God sent forth his Son, made of a woman, made under the law." The message remains the same: In the fulness of time, according to his timetable, God sends forth his Son to meet us where we are, as we are, and whoever we are. Unfortunately, those who work for Christ are often the first to mold their own agenda. When that happens, God has interesting ways of reminding us of the sovereignty of his timetable, as the following story shows.

I arrived at O'Hare at 8 A.M., checked my bags, and boarded the plane, a 727 headed for Detroit. Having flown on nearly every model of commercial aircraft, I have learned some of their peculiar characteristics. The 727 fascinates me with its quick ascent on takeoff. Not this time. By the time we left the ground, I was counting numbers at the end of the runway. Once airborne, smoking privileges were restored and it appeared to be a normal flight. After a westerly departure we swung back over the suburbs and the city and headed across the lake. I was enjoying a magazine when the announcement came: "Please fasten your seat belts and return your tray tables to an upright position. We are returning to O'Hare. *Click.*" The guy beside me lit three cigarettes at the same time. It was 8:30 A.M., but some dude in the back of the plane was screaming, "Bring me a drink!" My face flushed as the possibility of crashing registered. I looked out the window and all I could see was water. Pressing my nose against the window I thought, "What a way to go: just getting things together, people starting to listen and help, twenty-eight years old—it's too soon. And what about Celeste and the kids?"

I glanced at the people around me. The original shock was over, and a stilted quiet filled the cabin. Turning again to the window, I prayed—partly because I couldn't do anything else, partly because I needed it.

Lord, you've been good to me. I can't really remember any tragedies in my life (I hope this isn't the first). I can remember a bunch of victories and I'm thankful. If this is the end (the thought seems so remote), take care of Celeste and the kids."

My nose remained against the window as we descended over Chicago and landed. It was over, and I was embarrassed at my yellow streak. Two weeks later an airline mechanic who was a member of our church told me about a flight to Detroit that was saved from crashing by one lug-nut. He laughed uncontrollably when I recounted my experience. I didn't think it was funny at all.

Through the unfolding of circumstance God reveals his will and underlines his sovereignty. By measuring day-to-day events in that light, we discover a new method of hole-knocking.

Chapter Three

The Light in Hope

Dudley was a loyal dog. He would do anything to keep us happy. While still in school, we were living in an off-campus apartment and decided it was time to have a pet. The classified ads indicated an address where mutts were being given away, and Dudley came into our life. He was a little black character with a brown nose. He was also a lover. He was also smart. That pup went everywhere with me. I had a '54 Cadillac convertible at the time, and Dudley would perch on the seat beside me and co-pilot every venture. He went to class, the library, the billiard room—you name it, Dudley was there.

When we moved to our first parish he was part of the package. Of course, the kids took to him right away, and he enjoyed such niceties as his own birthday party, all scraps from every potluck supper, and the convenience of the church shrubbery. He particularly delighted in doing his tricks (shaking hands, playing dead, sitting, and rolling over) for our parishioners.

Each morning Celeste would get up and let him out the back door. Within five or ten minutes he would be scratching to return. His next duty consisted in getting into bed with me and convincing me of the deeper value of ministerial tasks as compared to the warmth of the bed. He was rarely unsuccessful.

Obedience came easy to him because he was so affectionate. It took only a slightly raised voice to send him cringing into the nearest corner. His most obvious trait was sensitivity. A timely frown would result in a tail-between-the-legs, chin-on-the-floor position of contriteness. Still, his desire to be loved did not dampen his spirit of adventure. This proved his undoing.

It was a Saturday morning, and Celeste had already let him out when I heard her shout, "Dudley Johnson, you get back here this minute!" I didn't even have to look. I knew what had happened. He had crossed the road in front of the house. For some reason, I also knew what was going to happen, and I tried to stop it. I ran to the front window and saw him running full tilt for home. He wasn't about to be cautious—he was too busy being obedient. The car was moving too fast to stop or swerve, and it hit him squarely, sending him spinning into the ditch. As I pulled on my pants, I could hear him howling. Celeste got to him first and carried him to the car as I was starting it. There were no external injuries and we thought he had a chance. He thought so too, and he quieted down as soon as Celeste picked him up. I can still remember him looking up at me as I drove frantically to the vet's. The first one was closed. The second was busy, but he recognized the emergency and examined our friend immediately. "Extensive internal damage. Leave him and I'll call you if anything happens." Two stunned people went home to wait and hope.

Hope is trying to do one thing while your mind is on another. Hope is talking, smiling, laughing, and planning on the outer level, while at gut level you care about just one issue. Hope is going to the hardware store and talking about the Chicago Bears, with images of a little black dog burning in your mind. Hope is charging through the door with one question: "Did they call?" The negative answer is good because you can keep hoping; nothing is final. Hope is deliberately letting the phone ring three times before you pick it up and hear "Your dog is dead."

Three days later I would find myself sitting on the couch crying over a silly little dog. Crying because the hope was gone.

The hole in the ceiling tells us that the hope is never gone. It tells us that, when we can dig up the courage to look, the love of God can even penetrate an unwanted phone call.

As a child I was taken in by the fabulous offers on breakfast cereal boxes. One time, during my third-grade year, I ordered a model F-86 Sabrejet from a company in Battle Creek, Michigan. (I remember because I was home for three-quarters of the school year with rheumatic fever.) For me, the big moment came every day between the hour of 10 A.M. and 12 noon. Every day I was sure the mailman would bring my Sabrejet. The jet took nearly six weeks to arrive, and when it came I was doubly disappointed. First, because it was a cheap, paper replica. And second, because I knew I couldn't look forward to tomorrow. The issue was final. Settled.

By contrast, in the Resurrection we find hope in finality. It is over. It is historical fact. And because it is, we have hope. We are free to dream, free to fabricate, free to search and reach and grow. And the hole in the ceiling gets bigger as we wrap our lives in hope. This is particularly true when the frailty of our humanity is illuminated.

There are certain words that have special meaning for me; words like *love, shut in, sacrament, unanimous, yes,* and *vacation* all strike special chords. But the most loaded word is *terminal.* God knows how much I despise that word. Yet, as I have tried to minister in terminal situations, I have learned to truly appreciate the promise of **life with Christ. There is something about finality that** makes us hope more and live better. Our values seem to rise to a higher and more meaningful level.

When faced by sure defeat, we stop worrying about victory and start caring about dignity.

When faced by death, we release our grip on the temporal and take note of the eternal.

When faced by loss, we smother our greed and celebrate what we still have.

This is the nature of hope—to leap barricades, to befuddle the witches, to outsmart the tyrants, to conquer despair. Perhaps the wisdom of God was never more clear than in the question mark that hovers over the Resurrection. Nobody has it ice cold. Nobody has a fixed formula. We have God's Word, and it is the anchor of our hope. On a purely rational basis the Resurrection is nearly impossible to swallow. This was Thomas' problem. I like to refer to him as an "IBM Christian." He wanted to see the computer write-out before investing his dreams in the product. But to play that game is to destroy hope, as Thomas' friends managed to convey to him when they convinced him that he must come to the upper room. To practice hope one must place oneself in the receiving position. One must be open to the unexpected. By going to the upper room, Thomas allowed himself to be surprised. At the same time the hole in his ceiling brought forth a new light and a new conviction. The point is, it never could have happened if he had not been free to hope, even in a skeptical way.

So many times we program ourselves away from hope with negative attitudes. "It can't happen here," "Our people are too sophisticated for that," "It's too late"—all of these reflect the refusal to hope. They also reflect the resignation to fail. They have no place in a faith that is based on a resurrected Lord.

The trick is to discipline yourself to dream. I once had a friend who was facing the trauma of brain surgery. X rays indicated that Harry had a tumor the size of a grapefruit. The day of surgery came and I made my way to the hospital. He was already on the operating table when I arrived, and I met his wife coming out of the chapel. To my amazement she was all smiles. This baffled me, as I had talked with the surgeon and learned that the chances of her husband's survival were slim and it was almost a sure bet that if he lived he would be partially paralyzed. I had gone to comfort the sorrowing, and I found myself stunned by a celebrant. It was unreal.

"I have just met with the Lord and I know that everything will be OK," she said. Fearing a letdown, I took the Thomas part: "Don't get your hopes too high. We must be ready for everything." In reply she whispered, "I am ready for everything. It's what I have asked for."

Two weeks later, her husband was walking around his home waiting to go back to work. To hope is to ask for everything, fully expecting to get it.

This does not mean that we always get everything we request. It does mean that we must make our petitions in hope, and mold our attitudes to accept God's answers as victories. Even if they fall short of our dreams. I'm sure that wonderful woman would have been thankful for God's love regardless of the outcome. Why? Because her hope was anchored in God's will and not her own. If her husband had died she would have been thankful for his peace. If he had been partially paralyzed, she would have praised God for sparing his life. And when he emerged completely whole, she credited the hand of God in the skill of the surgeons. She hoped for everything and she was ready for everything. Her hope was open-ended, and that was its strength.

So it is with the Cross. It gives us an open-ended, all-inclusive hope. In dying for all of us Christ granted every one of us a full-fledged title to hope.

Would that each of us could be blessed with such a glorious outlook on life that every time we got hit in the face we could consider the source and rejoice in it. The hole in the ceiling is most accessible when we veil it with hope: hope that is anchored in the historical resurrection of the Son of God; hope that transcends pain and disappointment; hope that is eternal.

Early in the sixties a Chicago-based religious organization built a theological system on the belief that all the great theology of the twentieth century had already been written. To be so bold as to limit the creative influences of the Holy Spirit is a grave mistake indeed. Even as they were taking their daring stand, the foundations were being undermined by a brilliant German theologian called Jürgen Moltmann. His *Theology of Hope* may well be the most significant work not only of this century but of the next as well. The role of the eternal promise manifested in Jesus Christ is at the heart of his work. It is also at the heart of Christianity itself. All this challenges us to look ahead hopefully.

The biblical scriptures are not a closed organism with a heart, or a closed circle with a centre. On the contrary, all the biblical scriptures are open towards the future fulfilment of the divine promise whose history they relate. The centre of the New Testament scriptures is the future of the risen Christ, which they announce, point forward to and promise.[2]

If we believe in a resurrected Lord, if we accept the power of God to conquer death, if the love of God can overcome the limits of man, then we must begin to let it show in our **lives. The hole in the ceiling will yield little light as long as** we are bent on returning to the good old days. We've been there already. We don't need or deserve God's guidance to repeat the past. But when we concern ourselves with the newness of tomorrow and the reality of a God who lives with us *now,* we are permanently bound to God's will as he shows it to us. In the *hope* provided in the Resurrection we are given a means of illuminating a free and wholesome life-style. This is the universal element in the Christian faith that gives us all equal ground on which to build. Unfortunately, most current Christian writing is concerned with winners. But what about those ventures that come up short? What about the average people who work the eight-hour shifts, question the sanity of TV program producers, and worry about the way their kids are growing up? How does the Christian faith offer them anything special?

It does so through hope. Hope is the one ingredient of the faith that carries equal weight for the winner, the loser, and the ordinary person. When Jesus Christ blasted the limits of man's experience by conquering the tomb, he provided a vision for all men. He set a goal that all of us can reach for, regardless of social status, intellectual capacity, or political connections. God intervened in history in a way that no man can fully comprehend. We all stand in awe at that deed. And in that moment of stunned wonder, we become one in him. The hole in the ceiling gives forth a universal light that can transform our attitude from drab endurance to electric expectancy.

The return of the American POWs from Vietnam raised some serious questions in the minds of thoughtful Christians. Reading of the terrible living conditions, physical discomfort, and lack of medical attention, we are sickened. But most mind-boggling of all is the idea of as much as five years of solitary confinement. Think of that.

Alone, no sharing, no listening, no telling for five years. What does man cling to under circumstances like those? There is only one answer: *hope*. It is the only way to overcome despair. Ultimately, it is the key to finding meaning in our existence. It reaches beyond meaninglessness with the promise of love.

I was stricken with rheumatic fever twice: once in third grade, and again in the fifth. Thus for my sixth-grade year I found myself attending the Special Education School at Illinois State University. It was one of the most significant years of my youth. Daily rest periods, special PE classes, and regular medication were only part of the package: the real therapy came from living with kids who were hurting more than me. Our room included kids suffering from the effects of polio, muscular dystrophy, heart disease, and just about anything else you can think of. I was one of the most mobile members of the group.

There was one girl who holds a permanent place in my memory, mostly because of the hope that filled her life. She suffered from muscular dystrophy and was confined to a wheelchair. Her hands moved in a quick, jabbing fashion, and she drooled when she talked. Understanding what she was saying was a major task even for the speech therapist. To put it briefly, she didn't appear to have much going for her. Wrong again. A more beautiful person I have rarely met. She could fall out of her chair with a grotesque thud and come up laughing at herself. Her sense of humor helped keep me in the principal's office most of the time. She would think up a deed and I would do it. They never believed me when I told them it was her idea. And she was always quick to share her personal belongings. More than once she ate only half a lunch. All of which is to say I learned to love her. But the thing I remember most about her occurred in her absence. It was during the spring of the year and I was running for secretary of the Student Council. I was searching for some cardboard to make a poster, when I found myself alone in the therapy room. It was almost noon and everyone had left for lunch. My friend had been the last one to use the walking bars. I knew that when I saw a single word in her scribbly handwriting scrawled on the blackboard at the end of the walkway. It's a great word, and I never hear it that I don't think of her. The word was *maybe*.

The hole in the ceiling explodes when at the moment of despair and defeat we can say, "Maybe." To hope is to remain oblivious to apparent loss and say, "Maybe." It is the promise of the empty tomb.

Chapter Four

The Light in Freedom

Perhaps the most essential ingredient for spotting the hole in the ceiling is the freedom to look. It's not that easy—particularly if, like me, you've been preconditioned to believe yourself unworthy of God's love.

Middle Tennessee State University is located in Murfreesboro, a sleepy little town loaded with tradition. And Tennessee is far enough south that some of its inhabitants refuse to concede that the Civil War is over. So when I scheduled a program for the interfaith group on the campus, I was somewhat unsure of my welcome. "Chicken" would be a good word for the way I felt.

I was wrong. Some of the most honest searchers I have ever met surfaced at M.T.S.U. In fact, the atmosphere was so fruitful that we scheduled "firesides" for each evening after the program. During these informal moments we talked about a myriad of live issues: premarital sex, abortion, scriptural authority, amnesty, and the continuing war in Vietnam. Candor abounded, and I am sure that my latent dogmatism was evident.

One evening, as I sat by a fireplace with a handful of three-by-five question cards in my hand, my attention strayed from what I was saying to the expressive face of an attractive coed. Concern puckered her forehead, and I felt her frustration when I looked into her eyes.

"What's the problem?" I asked.

Glancing away, she mumbled, "Too free!"

That baffled me. "Why?"

Her answer could be echoed by many who have given up their individuality for the faith: "I've always believed there are certain things a Christian can't do. You know— like smoking, drinking, gambling, and all that stuff. But if I hear you, you're saying that a Christian can do anything."

She heard me. I do indeed believe that if we are truly saved by Christ's sacrifice, then we are free to do as we wish. A Christian can do anything—and still be accepted by God. The point is, there are some things that a Christian won't do, because he is accepted by God. Fortunately for some, unfortunately for others, what it is that a Christian won't do because of his acceptance by God cannot be determined by someone else. The freedom to decide for yourself what your life-style will be is pivotal to perceiving the hole in your ceiling.

Contrary to first appearances, I am not endorsing an irresponsible, reckless, carefree style of life. In the fullest context of being a Christian, free will demands responsibility.

One of the freest spirits I have ever encountered was a high school chum by the name of Paul Grimes. This guy was totally uninhibited. After observing him for just a few moments, most people felt gifted in their sanity. One Sunday morning my brother and I were homeward bound—having already made the trek to church—when we saw Paul strolling down the street. We picked him up and drove on. Smack in the middle of Bloomington's plush country club estates, we noted that we had failed to get a newspaper.

"Pull over!" Grimes said.

"Are you nuts, Paul?" my brother replied. "You can't **get a paper here.**"

"Sure I can."

We pulled over to the curb. Paul climbed out and trotted across the manicured lawn of a beautiful, collonaded Georgian home. He rang the bell, looking like a delivery boy standing there in his cutoffs, sweatshirt, and sneakers. A lady opened the door and stood amazed as Paul muttered something to her, proceeded into the living room, gathered up the pieces of the *Sunday Pantagraph,* and scampered back to the car, where my brother and I were convulsed with laughter. As we drove away, paper in hand, I looked back and saw the man of the house furiously shaking his finger in his wife's face. Call it nerve, call it brass, or call it obnoxious—regardless, it takes a lot of freedom to pull off such a stunt.

Grimes could do it because he was confident he could deal with any eventuality. If the husband had thrown him out, he would have laughed. If the woman had screamed, he probably would have apologized. My guess is that as he crossed the lawn he considered all the possibilities. Then he took control of the situation.

So it is with anyone who seeks to be free. It's not a matter of "doing your own thing" and shirking the responsibility. Rather, to be fully free is to assess the situation, weigh the options, measure your motivation, *act,* and be willing to take responsibility.

As a kid I experienced this responsibility in an unforgettable fashion. It happened when I was thirteen and in love. That is a formidable combination—and even more so when your parents take a trip and leave both a pickup truck and a set of keys at home. Having never driven the vehicle before, I was a little shook when I turned the key on that fateful Saturday.

We lived about four miles from the village of Downs, where a junior high basketball game was being played that very afternoon. My love was a seventh-grade cheer-leader, and my plan was to drench myself with Old Spice, slip into the truck, cruise down there, and casually blow her mind. It almost went beautifully. After backing the truck by fits and starts (the clutch was alien to me), I managed to get onto the highway. The gears worked easier than anticipated and I was on top of the world. I remember whistling to myself and hanging my left arm out the window just to look cool. I *was* cool—until I tried to make a turn. It was at least a forty-five-degree corner. You can't do that at fifty miles an hour. I tried.

The skid marks measured over sixty feet. To go into a ditch is one thing. To go into it with such force that you become a part of it is still another. The left front fender was mangled, the headlight smashed, and metal pressed against the wheel so it wouldn't budge. My body wasn't hurt; my ego was deeply wounded. There is an excellent chance that I would still be in that ditch were it not for a dear man (I don't know his name to this day) who fetched a rope and pulled the fender away from the tire.

At that point I was in love no longer. All I wanted to do was get the truck home. As I drove back up the road my mind hummed with thoughts of the punishment awaiting me. Reasoning that things would go easier if they didn't know I had ventured onto the highway, I decided to wreck the thing again—at home.

Just two days before this incident, a new gravel drive-way had been poured from our home, which sat on a hill, down to the stable some two hundred yards away. I gin-gerly negotiated that pathway and spotted an oil drum standing by the stable. It tumbled as the truck hit it.

I ran across the lawn to the home of my best friend. Ron Hastings was the same age as me and a partner in all my juvenile crimes. He was a Dick Tracy kind of kid who thought of everything. It was no surprise to me when he demanded the right to inspect the damage and help me fabricate a story. Today, I know I would have fared better without his counsel.

With me standing in ashen-faced silence, Ron stalked around the truck scratching his chin.

"This won't work. He won't believe it," he stated flatly.

I was incensed. "What do you mean, he won't believe it?"

Ron beckoned me. "Come here, stupid. Just look at the truck." A pause. "Now, look at the oil drum."

He was right. The oil drum didn't have a scratch on it. The decision was mutual: we started to search for something bigger to run into.

Every good farmer knows that when fencing is installed there is at least one post that is super-solid. It has to be: the rest of the fence is stretched to it. To our delight, we found that post nearest to the stable, adjacent to the driveway. A pile of left-over gravel separated our target from the stable. It was perfect.

We backed the truck to the top of the hill and started down.

"You goin' any faster?" Hastings asked.

"Yep!"

He was gone. The door was still open. I got about twenty feet from the post, concluded that I didn't want to see what I was going to do, and proceeded to lie down in the seat.

The truck snapped that post like a toothpick, hit the mound of gravel, flew eight feet in the air, hooked a fender on the roof of the stable, ripping it free, smashed through the end stall, and came to a smoking halt jammed between what was left of the stable and the paddock.

Hastings stood wide-eyed and horrified as I climbed

out of the wreck. When I reached his side, he dropped a classic: "Man, he's gonna believe this!"

Four hours of agony followed as we huddled in the basement waiting for my folks to return. When they arrived we could hear my dad bellowing as he came through the door, "Where's the truck?"

I met him at the top of the stairs. It was one of those incomparable encounters between a father and son.

"Where's the truck?"

"Down at the stable."

"What's it doing there?"

"It's stuck."

"Where?"

"Between the stable and the corral."

"It won't fit."

"I know."

My dad swung around to go look at the ruins. My mother, always the diplomat, shooed me off to bed. I quivered for forty-five minutes waiting for Dad to come. He never did.

The next day we went to church: no conversation. The day passed. Monday I went to school, then basketball practice. Afterward, Dad picked me up and never mentioned the truck. Back at home I sat down for supper— and discovered a folded piece of paper on my plate. It was a bill for $684. It was also my summer.

Anyone who has ever been tempted to cut loose can identify with that story. It always prompts "when I was a kid" responses. The moral is unavoidable: all of us have the right to embark on self-centered, daring adventures. But when we do, we must be prepared to foot the bill. Accountability is the guardian of freedom. Experience has taught me that my independence is determined by my willingness to be responsible for my actions.

While I had a parish, I had the strongest urge to march down the aisle some Sunday morning clad in a sweatshirt and Levis. It would have been gimicky, but a great way to talk about plastic, "Sunday-best" Christianity. By chance, I shared my scheme with our youth director, Dick Payne, and some of the high school kids during a weekend retreat. Their reaction expanded the hole in my ceiling. To my amazement, they were appalled. Being a close friend, Dick told me straight, "It would be out of place and you couldn't deal with the consequences."

Dick's remark freed me (in this instance) from one of my most stubborn bondages—impulsiveness. There is a great difference between impulsiveness and freedom. By making me consider the effect, he had peeled the glitter from the cause. I believe this is the point of Paul's emancipation proclamation, "For freedom Christ has set us free; stand fast therefore, and do not submit again to a yoke of slavery" (Galatians 5:1 RSV). Madcap actions are powerful slave-masters. They also shroud the hole in the ceiling. Christian freedom calls for the guts to take your hands off the controls and wait for God's action. I shudder to think of the times when I have impulsively blocked the light of God's love through my own haste.

It happens when I rationalize my way into trading a car (I get the fever) and end up with a lemon. Or when I shout at my son for something my daughter did. Or again, when I misread somebody's facial expression, think they don't like me, and never give myself the chance to love them. In every case, I am the loser. I am bound by the shackles of my impulses. Authentic freedom comes from accurate evaluation, long-range planning, responsible action, and—most of all—the peace of knowing that even when I blow it, God won't.

Emil Brunner picks up this theme in *The Divine Impera-*

tive. His succinct statement knocks the props from under those who would reduce Christianity to a pattern of social behavior. It also reveals the gigantic hole in his ceiling. "God Himself has taken away from man all anxiety about himself, He Himself has settled the account. Man's life is secure in God. To believe means: 'Don't bother about yourself any more!' God has put all your affairs in order. Whoever lives in faith, in justification, is free from all anxiety about the 'I.'"[3]

That is the ultimate freedom that blasts a limitless hole in your ceiling; freedom from self-consciousness. As Arthur DeKruyter, senior pastor at Oak Brook's burgeoning Christ Church, put it, "If we only knew how much time others spend thinking about what we think, we wouldn't bother to think about it."

The credit card has had a tremendous impact in America. I am particularly susceptible (and my checkbook will back me up in this). For me it is much easier to fork over the little plastic credential than to release my grip on the green stuff. The pain of writing a check at the end of the month doesn't compare with the torture of breaking a ten-dollar bill. I realize this isn't the case with everyone, and it hasn't always been so with me.

At first glance, that credit card is a mind-boggling piece of freedom. If you can write your name, you can have anything. I suppose that's why I panicked when the bank charge cards first appeared. (Remember—they just printed them up and dropped them in the mail.) When mine arrived, I was horrified. I hadn't ordered it. As soon as I saw it I broke out in a bankruptcy rash. No way was I gonna carry one of those. I chopped it up and threw it in the trash. Why? Because I couldn't cope with the responsibility it required.

So it is with those who prefer a faith defined by dos and

don'ts. They need limitations because they are horrified by the freedom Christ has won for them. Their faith is none the weaker; that's just where they are. The problem comes when they condemn others for not living the same way. Whether one likes it or not, there are people who can handle a credit card responsibly. The hole in their ceiling lets in enough light for them to keep things in perspective. So, too, some people can smoke, drink, and gamble responsibly, and it doesn't detract one bit from their faith.

What is freedom to one, however, can be disaster to another. Heredity is the difference. The point from which you begin your liberating journey will determine the road you take. I was excited by Dr. James McConnell's assertion that we must recognize the limits to our actions before we can conceive our freedom:

Everything you say or do is influenced by three things; (1) The way your body functions which includes the biological limits imposed by man's evolutionary experience with his environment; (2) Your personal experiences with an environment which taught you to act in particular ways; and (3) The environment you find yourself in which is really a range of specific stimuli that you react to.[4]

In other words, we are all limited by what our bodies can do, what experience has taught us, and how we react to specific situations. The joy comes when we discover through Christ that each of those limits (physical, environmental, and existential) can be broken.

This is the practical, freeing value of Christ's resurrection. In it he smashed history. He experienced something that destroys our limits, that makes us free and presents us with an awesome responsibility.

It is not easy to be free. On a plane where "thou shalt"

and "thou shalt not" carry no weight, we are left with a one-to-one relationship with God. To be consistent in that relationship is to measure all your actions against his unfailing love. It is to know that you are accepted as you are—and to grant others that same measure of acceptance. At that point the hole in the ceiling achieves fantastic proportions.

The best-selling novel *Jonathan Livingston Seagull* points to our tremendous hunger for freedom. In the narrowest context it could be called a blasphemous affront to the sovereignty of God. But in the widest sense, it is but a picture of what God intends for every one of us. I prefer the latter view, as it makes room for a new hole in my ceiling. Like millions of others, I saw myself in J. L. Seagull. He experienced failure that led to success. Ostracized by the crowd, he learned to fully accept himself. Filled with the joy of discovery—he sought to give it away. And, finally, he was left with the ability to love without thinking of the returns. That is freedom.

Chapter Five

The Light in Forgiveness

He wanted to be one up on his neighbors, but it was getting harder and harder to do. When he bought the Eldorado, they bought a Mark IV; when he put in a fifty-foot pool, they installed a seventy-five-foot one; and when he painted his house red, they painted theirs fuchsia. Then it hit him: the best way to score over his fellow Pharisees of Jerusalem Estates would be to invite the rabble-raising preacher Jesus over for dinner. That would do it for sure. Simon reached for the phone.

"Hello, Jesus?"

"Yeah."

"What's happening?"

"Nothing."

"Got a date for dinner?"

"No."

"Like chop suey?"

"It's OK."

"How 'bout joining me for supper?"

"Right!"

At 6:30 Christ arrived. Of course he was driving a Volkswagen and the neighbors were appalled by his presence. The dinner wasn't three minutes under way when the doorbell rang. Simon opened the door and nearly choked. Standing before him—in painted splendor—was a woman of the streets. She walked right past him, through the living room, and into the dining room, where

56

Jesus was eating an egg roll. Kneeling at his feet, she proceeded to bath them with her tears, dry them with her hair, and anoint them with expensive perfume. It blew Simon's mind. You see, he knew who she was as soon as he saw her (an interesting insight to the "other" side of Simon), and now he couldn't believe the Master would actually let her touch him.

The Lord spoke. "Simon, once there were two men who borrowed money from a rich friend. One took fifty dollars, the other five hundred. Shortly after the deal was concluded, the loaner made a killing on the stock market and decided he didn't really need the money he had lent. He called both of the borrowers and told them to forget it. Now, Simon, which one would love him more?"

Without hesitation the miserly Pharisee answered, "The one who was forgiven most."

My guess is that Christ smiled at him then. He had him. The recorded rebuke rings with sarcastic truth: "Even so, Simon, this woman, who has been forgiven much, loves much in return. When I entered your home you didn't even give me water for my feet; *she* washed them with her tears and dried them with her hair. Your kiss of welcome never came; *her* kisses have fallen on my feet since she arrived. And you never offered oil for my head; but *she* has covered my feet with perfume. Simon, those who are forgiven little, love little in return. But those who are forgiven much, love much in return."

The simple truth behind that incident gives us a new hole in the ceiling. Motivation to love can be found in forgiveness. In fact, if the forgiveness is genuine, love is inevitable.

But how do we measure forgiveness? How do we know when we are fully forgiven and forgiving? What is the difference between forgiveness anchored in love and manipulation in pursuit of love? And, is it possible to separate ourselves from God's forgiveness?

If the ultimate example of forgiveness is the Cross, there is only one principle by which to measure forgiveness. *True forgiveness never includes a contract.* In other words, when we really forgive we never include an "if."

During my college years I had a running battle with the idea of forgiveness. Wheaton College is a conservative school—so much so, that each semester students are asked to sign a pledge regarding their social behavior. When I was there this consisted in promising to forego smoking, drinking, card-playing, movie-going; dancing, and belonging to any secret society. Initially I had no problem with this. In fact, during the first three months I developed my own brand of Pharisaic righteousness. I can still remember the questions of my high school friends when I was home for vacations: "You sure have changed, what's it like?" or "What *do* you do for fun at Wheaton?" I would humbly explain the necessity of choosing a life-style for Christ, and they would condescendingly smile and walk away. The problem was, I really didn't believe that such social abstinences had a damned thing to do with Christianity; I was just doing what I was told. That lasted for almost a year. Then, I started hitting an occasional flick, sharing a beer with friends, and enjoying clandestine rendezvous with my pipe. All this resulted in an agonizing guilt complex. I would pray for forgiveness on my way home from the theater, smash beer cans, and literally throw pipes away (I must have pitched a hundred dollars worth of pipes).

Then Don Moomaw, a Presbyterian preacher, came to campus. He was preaching a series of evangelism meetings, and one of my housemates asked him to come visit us. (Most of the guys were ditching the meetings and this was the only way he would get to them.) He arrived at 11 P.M. That impressed me. He was obviously pooped from a full day of student pummeling, and he had to get a message ready for the next morning; but he still came and he stayed well into the morning. During the course of the conversation he told a story that changed my life. He didn't know it. In fact, he was talking to one of the other guys—but I was listening.

It seems that a father returned home from work to find a bucket of paint dumped upside down in the garage. With a wife and a six-year-old son, he had little difficulty guessing the likely culprit. After cleaning up the mess he went in for supper. Midway through the meal the father pondered aloud, "Gee, I wonder who dumped the paint out in the garage?" The boy just kept eating, never looking up. After supper, as he was reading the evening paper, the father repeated the question. Again the boy acted as if he never heard a thing. Shortly thereafter, the father felt a hand on his knee. When he moved the paper aside he was confronted with a tear-streaked face, and his remorseful son confessed, "Daddy, I dumped the paint out in the garage."

At that point, Moomaw stopped the story and asked his listeners some questions. What did the father do? Did he slap the kid in the face? Did he scream at him? Did he kick him? Did he banish him to his room? No way. He picked him up, sat him on his kee, and explained that everybody blows it once in a while. When we do, the best thing to do is clean up the mess and keep going. Then came the power line: It's the same way with Jesus Christ. He knows that we're just people; we're gonna blow it time and again. When we do, he asks us only to clean up the mess and keep going. His forgiveness of us is complete. We live in a state of perpetual forgiveness. The Cross is a historical fact. It is finished. Unfortunately, we have failed to interpret it in such a way that all persons can grasp its significance. The Good News is joyously simple. We are forgiven. No matter what we do, God's grace is sufficient to remove the weight of our fault. At Calvary God made an eternal statement: *I love you* . . . period.

On this premise conditional forgiveness is impossible. There is no "if."

I learned what unconditional forgiveness is as a kid. We had a dog that was an incorrigible car-chaser. More than once I was greeted by the sight of a policeman's three-wheeler parked at the back door when I came home. That meant that Spink had done it again. She delighted in chasing motorcycles. The dog was six years old when we moved to a house in the country on a state highway. She was not stupid. The fast traffic didn't even tempt her. She knew better. Her infamous habit was satisfied by a blacktop road adjacent to our property. The toll exacted from all who used that road was fifty yards' pursuit by a yipping white dog. Time and again we punished her, but no matter what we did, given the opportunity she would chase again. She died doing it. And I cried as I dug her grave and buried her wrapped in my bedspread. Love can't be destroyed by disobedience. Forgiveness never includes a contract.

But what happens when there is a contract?

Contracts build walls. They destroy perspective. And they eliminate the possibility of fully trusting relationships.

Consider the child who is caught in the cookie jar. My son is presently in the twilight weeks of the "terrible twos." He likes cookies and he can scoot a chair through the kitchen without making a sound. The cookie jar is never full. Of course, we have sought to limit his con-

sumption, and, again, I have learned to practice forgiveness, the classic line being "If you take one more cookie,
you're gonna get a licking." Being his father's son, that is
no deterrent to Dane. It's a challenge. Can he get the
cookie? Will he really be spanked? When should he try?

By imposing the contract, we have encouraged the act.
If he has any sense of selfhood, he has to try. So it is with
any kind of forgiveness based on an "if."

This principle is particularly applicable to those who
find it impossible to forgive themselves. By constantly
resurrecting their failures they only multiply the possibility of new blunders. The hole in the ceiling appears when
we accept the fact that we are already forgiven and deal
responsibly with present circumstances. If there is no
threat there is no issue.

Frank Ivey was caught in a lingering love affair. His
wife was fully aware of it. She didn't threaten him. She
didn't harp on his infidelity. She simply reinforced her
own faithfulness. Regardless of what he did, she was still
there. When he finally realized that she loved him
enough to forgive—not just verbally, but through
psychological and physical constancy—he changed the
circumstances and terminated the destructive relationship. There was no contract, no "if." His wife was just
there. It took time, patience, and a good deal of prayer
support, but her acceptance of him in his incomplete state
ultimately made him whole. Forgiveness works that way.
Its therapeutic power comes not from the threat of
punishment but from the steady presence of grace.

My childhood was dotted with grace-pervaded incidents. Parental discipline was not lacking, but I always
had the feeling that, regardless of my actions, I would be
loved. This does not mean I was loved for my mistakes.
Rather, I was loved in spite of them. I remember the

occasion of my first real bow and arrow. It was my tenth birthday, and my dad had given me five dollars to buy an archery set. In retrospect, I am sure he envisioned arrows with suction cups. He looked a little startled when I returned with a ten-pound-test archer's bow and two field arrows. At the time, his sign shop was located in a large garage behind our house. He was lettering a pickup truck when I appeared with the new bow, and he smiled in surprise at the size of my purchase (it was at least a foot taller than me). His index finger pointed as he instructed, "Be careful with that thing." Ten minutes later I loosed my first shot. It missed the tree for which it was intended, swooped through the window of the truck, and imbedded itself in the upholstery inside the driver's door. The woman who owned the truck was sitting in it. She fainted and I ran. As I recall, I scurried to "bum camp" (a transients' hangout near the railroad tracks three blocks from our house) and stayed there for the rest of the afternoon. As dusk fell, I knew I had to go home, and did, slowly. Both Mom and Dad were in the kitchen when I entered. "Welcome home, Robin Hood," my father said. "I had to give that job away to pay for the damages." Nothing else was said about the incident.

Today, my dad probably can't even recollect the episode. I will never forget it: not because of the action that was taken, but because of the lack of action. And that is the central ingredient to forgiveness. A certain hollowness comes through when the forgiver constantly emphasizes his action, either verbally or physically. That is bunk. When the forgiveness is real, it is once and for all. Continual reference to it betrays the absence of sincerity and the need for a power position.

I once attended a film festival in Chicago and saw a movie that crystallizes the point I am trying to make. The plot involved a love affair between a sensitive young girl and an egocentric boy. The strength of the picture lay in its portrayal of their developing relationship. It was warm and innocent. A second lad enters the picture when the boy leaves for a year of study. Upon his return he learns that the girl has had a child by her interim suitor. The child was released for adoption and the second lover is long since gone, so the original relationship is taken up again. But the strain is obvious. The boy cannot forget. The picture concludes with a forceful scene. The boy is lounging on the couch, and the girl is in the kitchen when he calls out, "Cindy."

"Yes?"

"I forgive you."

The last sound is the slam of the kitchen door as she walks out. The startled look on the boy's face is engraved in my mind. He deserved exactly what he got.

There are times when the words "I forgive you" mean nothing more than "I've got the upper hand." They are spoken to secure superiority and to exact payment for grace. So uttered, they are an insult.

Having contended with troubled marriages, alienated children, and enraged neighbors, I am increasingly convinced that real forgiveness involves little conversation and a lot of action. It's not easy and it consumes large chunks of time, but it enables both forgiver and forgiven to grow.

The hole in the ceiling brings hope and promise when we so lean on God's grace that we can personify the Calvary event for each other. That means being there all the time, accepting human folly, and making a concentrated effort to shut up and love.

With this understanding we can speak directly to the questions posed earlier in the chapter.

1. Forgiveness is best measured by consistent presence.

2. We know we are fully forgiven when we accept the eternal presence of God's love in Christ.

3. We sense the depth of our ability to forgive when we are willing to stop giving ourselves credit for the deed and to acknowledge the love of God as the enabler. Forgiveness anchored in love expects no return.

4. Regardless of our actions we can never escape God's forgiveness. The Cross is a historical fact.

Chapter Six

The Light in Growth

"You haven't changed a bit." When I hear those words, I see red. There is something insulting about labeling any person as the same yesterday, today, and forever. The mathematician John Von Neumann said, "To grow is to change. And to have changed often is to have grown much." Reflecting on the wisdom of those words, I feel confident in my assumption that an awareness of God's presence is directly linked to our ability to grow and to sense our progress. Certainly, one of the most obvious marks of sovereign love is the bestowed potential to grow.

Maxie Dunnam recalls an encounter with a betel nut box that heightened his understanding of Christian growth. While calling on an elderly lady he noticed the box sitting on an end table and commented on its beauty. As his hostess explained its origin he opened it. Both were amazed at the contents. Inside was a vacated cocoon and a dead butterfly. Maxie explained that the woman's grandson had obviously found the cocoon and placed it in the box. The life cycle culminated in the emergence of the butterfly. But, because he was boxed, the beautiful lepidopteran was doomed. That is a parable of growth.

I believe that every person is inherently beautiful like that butterfly. Similarly many of us must develop that beauty in spite of ugly surroundings. The potential is there in every person. Unfortunately, the possibility of being boxed in is as real to us as it was to the ugly cocoon. The result is the same: static, empty death.

Sensing the presence of God requires a continual effort to break out of our boxes and grow. That is not as easy as it sounds. In the box we find a pseudo-security. In the box we can be indifferent to the pain, confusion, and need of the outside world. In the box we can set our own agenda (game plan), and even though our effectiveness is stunted, we can convince ourselves of our rightness. I believe this is one of the primary reasons for the conservative nature of the institutional church. Having occupied itself with box-building for the last twenty years, it is now victimized by its own process. Even today, many of the most powerful and prosperous churches are capitalizing on the box-building principle. They demand radical commitment to a limited system, and, I believe, because of the apparent security offered, they have a magnetic appeal for a generation longing for solid ground. A sadness fills my heart when I realize that, regardless of motivation, in the box you die.

As I see it, one of the essential ingredients of Christian growth is the perception that following Christ means a process to be pursued rather than a position to be defended. For me, being a Christian means more than defining my doctrine and encircling myself with physical, psychological, and spiritual ramparts to fend off the assaults of a wicked world. On the contrary, I would prefer to drop my armor, come out of my clearly defined corner, and engage that wicked world on an hour-by-hour, day-by-day basis. My God is so real that I don't sweat. In fact, I am refreshed by his ability to illumine new situations and lead me on. Not everyone is willing to buy that life-style.

Recently I sat by a roaring bonfire in Ohio and conducted an open question session. Shortly after the discussion began, a young man proudly sporting the sweatshirt of one of the most fundamentalist universities in our country asked a question that merits our attention: "Are you born again?"

I was thankful it was a fireside meeting as I must have flushed. The question is a standard for those who want to witness in a predetermined fashion. The fact that I had just spent thirty minutes addressing the crowd about a Christian position on peace obviously didn't matter to the lad. Or else it mattered so much that he felt obligated to test the temper of my words. My response was not what he expected. I said, "A thousand times over."

There was a note of vindictiveness in that answer which I regret now. I do not regret the answer, for it is my firm belief that a growing faith demands renewed commitment every day. I can see no other way to deal with the unfolding of life. No one can predict the future. If we could, one well-defined commitment would be sufficient. But when the coming hour is as susceptible to calamity as it is to victory, there is a need for an adaptable faith and continual new commitment. To box yourself in the security of a prescribed life-style is tragically irresponsible. By limiting my responses to a given situation I curtail the wonder of God's creation. Yes, I am born again right now. I shall be born again tomorrow too.

That is what it means to view one's faith as process over against position. The process Christian is constantly moving, growing, risking, wrestling, changing. The position Christian is fighting a battle of entrenchment. His is a static life-style. Like the butterfly he may well grow in beauty; but unfortunately, because he chooses to box himself in frozen traditions and predictable situations, that beauty is shared only with those who are boxed in with him.

Again, I must make reference to the Incarnation. By becoming man in Jesus Christ God broke out of the box.

He placed himself in the process of life where he dealt with situations as they developed. Of course, there was a measure of risk. Because he would not conform to the box-builders of his time, Christ lost his life. Yet, even as he lost his life, he revealed the glory of being a whole person. That is the meaning of growth: forget your weaknesses and keep moving.

Bernie Grosso weighed 110 pounds in full football gear. He was a reserve halfback on our high school football team who survived on guts. He was easy to identify from any vantage point: he was the helmet running down the field by itself. Jack Plumber represented the other extreme. He looked like a football player—broad shoulders, thick neck, massive forearms. But whereas Grosso was fearless, Plumber was chicken. The little guy liked nothing more than smashing into a linebacker; Plumber shied away from contact. During one practice session the coach decided to prove a point. Leaving linebackers and backfield people to chuck mud balls at each other, he called the offensive and defensive lines together and set up a play. Grosso was to carry the ball. The plan was for the linemen to cooperate so that Grosso would end up one-on-one with Plumber. It worked, and the results were hilarious. When it was apparent that he would have to make a tackle the big guy secured his position, sat back on his heels, spread out his arms, and waited. Seeing that he was trapped, Grosso increased his speed, tucked the ball under his arm, put down his head, and barreled helmet-first into Plumber's midsection. Plumber was knocked cold. Grosso scored a touchdown. It all boils down to a choice between standing still and moving.

Those who practice a position type of faith, constantly defending and securing their predetermined attitudes, are often the first to collapse when confronted by a bumpy road. Having developed a machine-like system, they find it impossible to deal with unexpected developments. A death in the family, a bout with disease, a kid caught shoplifting, or a marital misunderstanding sends them whimpering to their knees. Suddenly, all the fixed patterns of behavior seem hollow, and there is a sense that God has deserted them. Like Plumber they can look good only until something hits them—then it's all over.

A life-style given to growth depends on flexibility. In assuming new tasks, responsibilities, and adventures the Christian must be willing to release his grip on past successes and tread in virgin forest. This calls for a healthy dependence on the Holy Spirit. In fact, when we accept the eternal presence of God through his Spirit, fear of the unknown loses its punch. I believe this basic confidence is what prompted Paul to write, in Romans 8:31, "If God be for us, who can be against us?" Somehow the hole in the ceiling casts more light when we consciously depend on it to light our way.

This is not to say that all a Christian needs to do in order to grow is to hang loose. No way. When I shake loose from my spiritual box I must do so with the knowledge that I will never have all the answers and will live in quest of new revelations from God. In that respect, Christian growth means not only the exchange of position for process but also a commitment to constant spiritual maintenance.

By the conclusion of the third round of the 1972 U.S. Open Golf Tournament, Jack Nicklaus had an unbeatable lead. As I recall, he was ahead by ten strokes with one round to play. He had it in the bag. No wonder those of us who watched the tournament were so amazed when the TV announcer opened the final broadcast by explaining that Nicklaus had spent the previous evening on the practice tee. He had it in the bag, but he wasn't satisfied. He wanted to get better.

The same is true of every Christian who recognizes that God's presence is illuminated by spiritual growth. Sure, the empty tomb boldly proclaims that we've got it made. We do. But we can always grow—and that means constant study, prayer, and people-contact. Without these, growth is out of the question.

When I speak of study I mean a wide realm of activity. Certainly Bible study enhances the life-style of the Christian. If a group can be formed with rotating leadership responsibilities, this impact is further increased. I have found that varying the theological positions also helps. Of course, ground rules that make room for each position must be adopted from the start. Yet another method of Bible study (this is good for the loner) involves selecting a particular biblical character, such as Peter, and tracing all references to him. Then, having completed your basic research, try to list the strengths and weaknesses of the subject. Conclude by comparing your own strengths and weaknesses with those of your biblical character.

Another method of study calls for a growing library. This isn't nearly as difficult as it used to be, for now Christian book clubs keep a constant flow of readable material available. In many cases, study guides and tapes are also procurable. I have found that just fifteen minutes each day is sufficient to cover at least one book a month. A word of caution is needed here. Some of the book clubs tend to put out books of consistently similar nature. Unless we watch the styles of our reading material, it is as easy to box our reading habits as it is our basic faith.

One of the mediums that I have used to vary my reading is magazines. At a time when journalism is severely threatened by lack of interest, it is mutually beneficial to take out a couple of subscriptions. Again, I cannot over-emphasize the need to seek a balance of theological positions. Those visiting my office are often bewildered to see *Christian Century, Theology Today,* and *Christianity Today* on the same coffee table. Each of these periodicals is a leader in its own field. I read and enjoy them all. I am persuaded that the state of the church (liberal, moderate, and conservative) would be fortified if we would all make it a habit to bounce new wavelengths off our minds through reading. It's also an exciting method of hole-knocking.

Prayer is another matter. I consider it not so much a hole-knocker as our way of acknowledging the hole. Like gently falling rain, it has a freshness about it that facilitates growth. I consider one of my greatest weaknesses to be my lack of a disciplined prayer life. By this I mean I don't have a patterned method of prayer, same time, same station, etc. For years I was a panic-prayer. Always aware that God cared about me, I didn't feel any real need to punch in everyday. So I didn't. My practice was to go like hell until I met trouble. Then, stymied, I would retreat, regroup my faculties, and pray for help.

Recently I have discovered just an inkling of what I was missing. I still don't make a practice of daily prayer, but now I pray more often and for different reasons. I pray to acknowledge God's goodness and to commit myself again and again to his future. I have learned that I can't control tomorrow, so I take great comfort in telling God, "Point me and push me, I'm ready to go."

A word must be said about prayer groups. Frequently I receive telephone calls soliciting my assistance in prayer chains. I must confess that I often wonder why I am so honored, but I always oblige. Furthermore, I am increasingly impressed by the depth of concern in the callers. Such concern bespeaks a sensitivity to other people that is a by-product of the prayer group. Regularly scheduled gatherings with the same people to evaluate and establish meaningful prayer often leads to deep personal relationships. That alone makes the prayer group a valuable experience.

This brings us to the third area of spiritual maintenance: people-contact. For me, this is the most testing and fruitful of all. It means a conscious effort to be where people are. One of the overarching themes of the New Testament is Christ's willingness to go to the marketplace, the shore, the well, the banquet, the funeral, the wedding, the temple. He met people where they chose to be—not necessarily where he wanted them. His consistent concern and presence, in spite of circumstance, sets an example for us. The hole in the ceiling grows bigger every time a Christian meets a new person. But we must be careful not to impose our agendas on others. Authentic witness has but one essential—to display the love of Christ.

Stan Roberts was a college associate of mine, and an inveterate "witnesser." On the Wheaton campus, his kind were a definite minority. His standard greeting was "How you getting along with the Lord?" There were occasions when it drove me nuts. Ten minutes before a final, the morning after a three o'clock session at the pool hall, or in the midst of a conversation with my fiancée, I really wasn't too concerned about my relationship with the Lord.

One winter morning I was driving a school bus down Roosevelt Road when a woman stalled her car right in front of me. I hit the brakes, but there was no way that a fifty-five passenger bus could stop. The I-Beam bumper smashed into the back of her car and sent it spinning into somebody's front yard. By the time I finished explaining to the police, the bus boss, and the school insurance man, I had already missed my first class. As I ordered a cup of coffee at the student union building, who should come floating up but Stan Roberts. "How you getting along with the Lord?" he greeted me.

My answer was prompted by the events of the morning: "Not worth a damn!"

I can still see Stan's tonsils. My apology and explanation calmed his horror and brought forth the genuine warmth that was his. Still, he never again greeted me with his stock formula. There is a valuable lesson there. As Christians, with knowledge of the overwhelming peace that comes from a day-by-day encounter with Him, it is a great temptation to greet others with bubbling joy. That's a mistake. More often than not, it turns people off and destroys God's opportunity to love through us. People-contact for Christ means caring first for the other person and his feelings. Once we have established where they are, the love of Christ makes its greatest impact if we meet them on their terms.

All of this makes for a life-style filled with risk. Without risk there is no growth. The world is filled with people with great ideas and potential. The only reason they have not risen to prominence is that they are afraid of jeopardizing what they have already. Christians seem to be specialists at this. With the security of acknowledging their acceptance in Christ there comes a natural tendency to freeze. It is as though we become so grateful for God's love in spite of our weaknesses that we would rather remain changeless than risk the possibility of new weaknesses through change. Such an attitude shows a tremendous lack of vision. I am continually awed by the fact that God's ability to love me for what I am refuses to let me sit still. In other words, acceptance in Christ is total; yesterday, today, and tomorrow.

I believe this is what Christ was saying to the disciples in the twenty-first chapter of John when he called to them from the shores of the Sea of Tiberias. They had been fishing all night, with no luck. Suddenly, the Master told them to change sides of the boat. It was such a simple process that we wonder why they hadn't done it earlier. But then, the nature of man tells him to do things the same way all the time. They probably always fished on just one side of the boat and depended on the drift to cover the area. Still, the Master said, "Change!" And when they did the results were fantastic.

Those of us who would be fishers for Christ might take note of this point. Maybe the hubbub of the sixties was his way of shouting, "Change sides of the boat." If so, we are just guts away from a burst of revitalization. There is but one barrier yet to clear: risk. If we do so in faith we may well experience the most phenomenal growth in the history of Christianity.

The only danger that I can see is the possibility of getting the means in front of the end. If prudence is not practiced we could well find ourselves worshiping change for the sake of change. Already there are some communities that have been turned into cults by this very process. It becomes an endurance contest. Finally, those who thrive on change and the extraordinary are the only ones left.

I suppose it might have worked the same way with the more impulsive disciples. Having experienced whirlwind success through change, they might have lost balance in pursuit of novelty. Christ knew this. That is why the conclusion of John's book reads the way it does, with Jesus revealing the governing principle to the most impetuous of the disciples, Peter. In concluding this chapter I want to lift up that principle.

After returning to shore and joining the Lord with

74

their bounty, the disciples built a fire, and a morning breakfast was prepared. As they were eating, Christ asked Peter three times, "Do you love me?" Each time the quick-tempered fisherman responded, "Yes"—the last time with a tone of irritation prompted by Christ's persistence. Each time, the Master challenged Peter's conviction with words of similar intent: "Feed my sheep," "Tend my sheep," "Feed my sheep." Therein is the principle that must govern all innovation. We are called to deal with people; to build bridges where walls have formed; to heal the wounds of indifference; to give hope to the despairing; to discipline ourselves to recognize our prejudices and hidden agendas for what they are and give shelter, guidance, and nourishment to the flock. Any change, alteration, or renovation that falls short of that standard cannot be the work of our Lord.

The only growth that knocks holes in the ceiling is that which furthers the pilgrimage of man.

Chapter Seven

The Light in Community

He sat directly in front of the window, both elbows resting on the sill, chin in his palms. A jaunty red roll-up cap perched on his head. Eric Sandholm was twenty-three. For the last twelve years he had been a patient in the fourth east ward of Elgin State Hospital. It was my pleasure to share worlds with Eric for only eight weeks. The impression his life made on mine is indelible.

At the age of eleven Eric accidentally shot himself through the left eye with a .22 rifle. The experience left him with a grotesque empty eye socket and a mind that plays between reality and fantasy. Basketball is his favorite activity. On the occasion of our first meeting Eric shattered my plastic chaplain's greeting, "Good morning, Eric, how you doing?" with a resounding "Go to hell." That was also the first time I ever saw the socket. My stomach knotted at the sight of it. Like an exclamation point thundering after his imperative it left me speechless. Three weeks later, after establishing a relationship with him, I brought him a black eye patch. In giving it to him I learned a valuable lesson. To begin with, he cried—with one eye. Secondly, he told me, "Nobody ever gave me nothin.' " But more importantly, he showed me a corner of humanness around which the Christian faith is built. With the patch perfectly in place, he stepped in front of a mirror, burst into a smile, and proclaimed, "Now I can talk to the girls."

Everybody needs to be needed. Even the guy destined to spin out his life in a state mental hospital. It is my conviction that the future of the church rests on our ability to comprehend that truth and mold a life-style around it. As we do so we will begin to form those communities in which the power of God can anchor itself. These communities will have a place for every person regardless of special gifts or talents. They will value persons more than program or property. Sensitivity to emotional extremes (high and low) will be their hallmark. They will keep a balance between celebration and intent and place a high priority on others' feelings. Their ceilings will be full of holes.

From the time I was old enough to comprehend the overtones of middle-class Christianity, I have felt I really didn't belong. Oh, I could play the game. I learned all the cute little phrases, and, although it taxed my self-discipline, I could also put on the air of quiet piety that so many of the local saints seemed to have mastered. But I didn't fit. I guess the best way to explain would be to say I wasn't satisfied. I didn't think I was better than the others. As far as I knew I was worse. It was just that the horizons of my dreams extended beyond resignation to life the way it is and thankfulness for the status quo. So I would fight myself to try and be what they were; to conform to the standards of Midwestern Anglo-Saxon conversatism. I couldn't do it. It wasn't me. Then I read the account of Saul's conversion and caught one phrase that filled me with hope. In response to Ananias' fear of dealing with Saul come the words "Go, for he is a chosen instrument of mine to carry my name before the Gentiles and kings and the sons of Israel" (Acts 9:15 RSV). God's willingness to use a killer left little doubt that he could use me. Indeed, he can use any person who is willing to be an instrument for him.

77

Keith Miller, in *The Taste of New Wine,* touches on that theme illuminatingly. Referring to himself as "a piccolo in the tuba section" he reveals his own sense of inadequacy. As he measured himself against the "good" people with whom he worshiped Sunday after Sunday, he built a 360-degree shadow around himself. From the tweeter of a stereo he might have found his freedom. Listening to a John Philip Sousa march, he could have heard the haunting tones of a piccolo. Even in the biggest band, there is a place for the piccolo. Our awareness of the presence of God increases as we make room for the piccolos all around us. Like Saul, every person is a chosen instrument of God. Stuck valves, broken strings, and cracked reeds notwithstanding, if we can join the band God will make music through us.

I witnessed the affirmation of a piccolo while I was doing a program in the heart of the Illinois farmland. I spotted him early in the evening. Dressed in tattered gray, he had a stubbly beard and a warm smile. He appeared to be in his early seventies. As the kids plunged headlong into the activities, there he was, right in the middle. Of course, his partner was called upon to wait occasionally, and help him move from time to time. But no one seemed to mind. In discussions he would stalk the subject, waiting until just the right moment to drop a concise sentence or two. Then, as his listeners digested his wisdom, he would flash a gap-toothed smile and glance around the circle. He looked like a misfit, but he was beautiful.

On the fourth night he slipped out of his group and joined me by the coffee dispenser.

"Barry, I want you to pray for me," he said.

"What's the problem?"

"I have to go all the way to Chicago tomorrow for X

rays. Somethin' to do with my lungs. I used to smoke a lot."

I had thought we were far enough from the circle that no one could hear. We were not. One of the kids heard it, and one of those simple, glorious moments of life was upon us. His group rose and formed a ring around us. Then, one by one, each of them (teen-agers, parents, and grandparents) uttered a prayer for the old man. As they prayed I looked at him. His head was bowed and he was quiet. Wet spots dotted the front of his shirt. The next thing I knew, the whole crowd had clustered around him and they were singing, "He's got the whole world in his hands . . . he's got Harry Palmer in his hands." Some weeks later I learned that the X rays proved negative. It was no surprise. If there was anything wrong with him, those people loved it right out of him that night. When we recognize everybody's need to be needed, such moments are multiplied and true Christian community is the result.

In trying to achieve communities structured on that principle, there are certain characteristics we should note. During the last three years our family has moved twice. Both occasions involved the search for a new church home. Consciously, we looked for a church that was fairly close geographically, took a moderate theological position, and showed signs of growth. Unconsciously, our standards were much higher. In retrospect this is how I see them.

1. A Priority on Persons Rather Than on Program or Property

I am especially sensitive about pushing programs on people. The only unsuccessful programs we have ever experienced developed after executive decisions. Since these came from the top down, there was no way the people would be open to our approach. On the other hand, our most satisfying experiences have come when the people all joined together to pull off the event. One of the marks of a healthy community is a basic respect for people, even if the program suffers as a result. People-oriented churches rarely have jam-packed calendars. They do have outstanding programs, but these are kept in perspective. The program is done *through* people instead of *to* them.

In the same sense, the healthy community doesn't dump all of its concern on a building. Note that I am not saying the building is unimportant. It is important, but only so long as it is available to the people. When the primary concern of the church is to glorify the edifice and keep adding "things" to it all the time, the community is sick. Most churchmen can painfully remember more than one board meeting when mundane material pursuits gobbled up 90 percent of the evening. That is a matter of misplaced priorities. I would favor time allowances to keep such folly under control; fifteen minutes for formalities, thirty minutes for material concerns, and forty-five minutes for people-oriented issues. The agony would come when we found ourselves unable to fill the last time slot. It would also tell us something about our church.

2. A Balance of Celebration and Intent

One of the most challenging weeks we experienced this past year came in a small Michigan church. The basic nature of our work is very joyous. We turn people on to celebrate their freedom in Christ. In most churches such an experience is welcomed and needed. But not always. The Michigan church was a case in point. A few years previously they had experienced another form of renewal through a lay-centered evangelism program. The result was a church that could celebrate. Decorating, singing, laughing, clapping their hands, and using guitar and tambourines were standard operating procedure. Unfortunately the celebration had little depth. After just one worship experience we knew we were faced with the exact opposite of what we normally encounter; whether it's plastic formality or plastic celebration, it's still plastic. Intent is the important thing. There must be a balance between the celebration and its cause. I grow restless whenever a practice becomes an end in itself. In a solid community there is a sense of spontaneity that lends itself to both the joyous and the solemn. By keeping the intent (the glorification of God and his creation) in mind, we can find a place for both. We spent the week in Michigan minimizing the party and maximizing the purpose.

The balancing intent and celebration is particularly difficult when we seek to repeat experiences. This has been evident wherever we have done a second program. In most instances, the style and tone of the first program are so refreshing that they set a standard against which every other program is measured, including EURISKON II. There is a decrease of festivity and an increase of content with the second program. More often than not this results in a few drop-outs. This is the price that must be paid if our first allegiance is to the gospel. The initial emancipating experience is but a means to an end. The end is a deeper, more committed, intent-filled personal encounter with Christ.

3. A Place for Individuals

The Christian community must be open to a wide variety of personalities, theological positions, and life-styles. I

81

am instantly suspicious of the congregation that talks alike, dresses alike, laughs alike, and gripes alike. Often these are the most powerful churches—at least outwardly. Their parking lots are filled with Buicks, Chryslers, and Mercuries, and their debts are all paid. Controversy is nonexistent because everybody knows what everybody wants. Those breaking the mold are coolly ignored and prayed for. But where is the healthy conflict of a church in mission? Who can be counted upon to question everything? What coalition challenges the administration and balances the program? Unless individuals are affirmed in their uniqueness, there is no tester's fire, and without this there is a blind parade.

I usually open our programs by giving credit to the theologians of hope for my operating base. If I am feeling insecure I will even drop the names: Moltmann, Pannenberg, and Braaten. That usually gives me a clear field, for few people are up on these writers. I did this once in White Plains, New York. After the service I was sipping a cup of coffee when a guy chugged right up and quoted two pages of *The Future of God.* I thought I'd die. The guy certainly had my number. After forty-five minutes of heavy point and counterpoint, he left. The pastor then informed me that the guy read everything and made it his mission to keep him honest. For the rest of the week I had a running exchange with this classic example of individuality. I grew. I think he did. And my mail tells me the whole church did. But it never could have happened without an open community that encourages every person to be himself.

The lost sheep comes to mind at this point as a timeless example of individuality. The rest of the sheep were groveling away eating yesterday's grass when he decided he couldn't hack it any more. He knew where the good stuff was and he went to get it. Of course, in the process he got hung up on a cliff, but so what? The issue is clarified when, after he exerts his independence and gets in trouble, the Master leaves the others and comes to him. The Lord is like that. He has a soft spot for the character who wants better grass. And when difficulty maroons the adventurer the Lord comes to him in his need and frees him to embark on yet another foray.

To me, one of the sure indicators of a vital Christian community is an abundance of characters. My awareness of the presence of God is intensified by a church filled with lawyers and bartenders, doctors and shoe salesmen, teachers and bricklayers, seamstresses and butchers. Match the vocational variance with theological contrasts, and I'll show you a hole-knockin' church.

4. Sensitivity to Need

This final area is difficult to describe, yet it is essential to a healthy community. I am talking about the ability to sense need both within the smaller community of the church and without. I recall hearing of an incident involving a young boy suffering from encephalitis. Since he lived in a small village all the neighbors were aware of his condition. When he took a turn for the worse, the local Methodist women's organization happened to be gathering to prepare a spaghetti dinner. Their leader asked that everyone pause and offer a prayer for the stricken boy. She was crushed when one of the ladies said, "I won't do that."

"Why not?"

"He's a Catholic, you know."

I have taken the liberty of using this negative example to point to a positive characteristic. A sensitive community pays no heed to doctrine, title, race, or dialect. If you're hurting—they'll be there. The putrid stench of discrimination doesn't fit in a community centered in Christ.

Late in the sixties many of the mainline congregations were confronted with the dilemma of taking a stand in the Civil Rights conflict. I consider it a sign of moral courage that so many of them chose to uphold the dignity of man as opposed to the security of their positions. Membership rolls dwindled and funds became scarce. It still stands as their finest hour.

In my own state there was a particularly outstanding case. A group of Black Panthers were falsely accused of a felony. That wasn't enough: their bonds were set ten times higher than was usual for such an offense. The local district of The United Methodist Church released the funds necessary to win their freedom. Although the money was never actually used, there was a rebellion within the church. Through it all the leadership stood firm. The issue was simple: human rights were being violated, and an unpopular but ethical stand was required. The prisoners were found innocent and released, and the funds were returned. Courage, dignity, sensitivity and concern for justice knocked a new hole in the ceiling.

The true test of Christian empathy is that it stems directly from Calvary and it stands as a goal that will ever exceed our grasp. As we consider the wider context of what it means to be a Christian community, we see that this ingredient is a must. Few of us would deny that the time on the cross was the darkest hour of our Lord, filled with pain, humiliation, and emotional agony. Still, as his life ebbed away he thought not of himself but of others: "Father, forgive them; for they know not what they do."

At the moment of our deepest grief, whom do we think

about—ourselves or somebody else? The ability to put the needs of others before one's own is the ideal toward which the Christian community can never stop striving.

My older brother, Bob, has always been a horseman. After he was drafted and I had gone away to school, my father was left at home with Mom and the two younger girls. Dad inherited the task of caring for Rebel, a once beautiful palomino who by then was twenty years old. Twice every day Dad had to feed him. If Reb hadn't been such a lovable old horse, Dad never would have done so; he wasn't too crazy about horses.

Shortly after my brother and I left home my folks adopted two more children, Mark and Marcy. When Mark reached the age of five he claimed Rebel. By now the horse was on his last legs: his hooves were split, his mane was straggly, and his back was swayed; but to the little kid, he was beautiful. One day while Mark was at school, Reb fell down and couldn't get up. By this time my brother had returned from the service and was living in an apartment in town, so they called him and he brought the vet over with him. A shot put the horse out of his misery. The problem was to get the horse buried before Mark got home from school. They didn't make it.

As soon as he got off the school bus Mark saw the action at the barn. Bob tried to stop him, but the little boy ran right past him to the side of his fallen horse. After a few moments of stunned silence, he looked up.

"Bob, Reb's not sleepin'?"

"No, Mark, Reb's dead."

After kissing the horse on the nose, Mark rose and walked head down to Bob's side. Not knowing what to do, Bob just stood there. Finally, he looked down at Mark's tear-streaked face. The five-year-old said, "Bob, you better let me tell Dad."

That story never fails to humble me. Christ said, "A little child shall lead them." This only proves the point: at the heart of the Christian faith stands the ability to think first of the other person. In face of this, doubting the presence of God seems ludicrous.

Chapter Eight

The Light in Selfhood

All this theory about awareness of God is worthless without a basic concept of the self.

Frank Reynolds gripped the edge of the table, his knuckles white. Inside him the tension jammed his guts together. The kid had been told at least five times to finish his beans. He was playing with them; nudging one behind the sugar bowl, flipping another toward the corner, burying still another under the potatoes. Smack! The sound of skin cracking against skin filled the kitchen. There was a moment of silence, then the piercing scream of a three-year-old. The left side of the boy's face flushed scarlet. Frank sat staring at his hand. For an instant he wanted to rip it off. But inside, he knew it wasn't the hand that troubled him, it was the temper. He had known about it for years—but he couldn't beat it. He thought himself a slave to it. Later, he would cuddle his son and tell him he loved him, and ache inside.

Not all of us are so fortunate as to have only a temper to worry about. All of us have some failing that reminds us of our humanity. Eating, smoking, gossiping, drinking, lying, gambling—the list is endless. The effect is the same. We can echo Paul's lament, "What I would I do not, and what I do I would not."

For me, the problem has always been my tongue. Ironic as it may seem, my most positive characteristic is also my most negative. I can remember feeling guilty for swearing when I was eight years old. I still do—both.

During the first year of EURISKON we conducted a survey to determine the subjects that people wanted to confront. On 85 percent of the forms returned, "self-understanding" ranked in the top three. Apparently, everybody would like to know why they live the way they do. In pursuing that subject I have discovered a tremendous hole in the ceiling.

Biblically, the problem is clearly universal. Both Old and New Testaments are jammed with incidents of self-searching. Job chastized himself demanding, "How many are mine iniquities and sins?" (13:23). David beseeched God, "Search me, O God, and know my heart: try me, and know my thoughts" (Psalm 139:23). And most meaningful to me, the disciples, in a dramatically convincing fashion, felt the same need. It happened at the Last Supper. The Master had announced that one of them would betray him. At that point, each of these men—men who had spent three years sweating, laughing, teaching, and learning with Christ—spoke up with the revealing question "Is it I, Lord?" Not a one of them knew himself well enough to predict his actions.

What this means to me is that total understanding of the self is out of the question. It is simply too much to ask, and Christ doesn't ask for it. In fact, he leads us away from such meaningless introspection with the challenge to cast all our cares—even the self-centered—on him.

Here I want to introduce a term that has loaded connotations. For years, the Christian community has avoided it, primarily because of its vagueness. We couldn't fully define it—so we ran from it. The term is *daimon*. In the sense that I want to use it there is no cause for alarm. Little red dudes with horns and pitchforks have nothing to do with it. Rather, it refers to that corner of man's nature that makes him impossible to duplicate and spiritually unpredictable. Rollo May devotes some twenty pages to defining it in *Love and Will*. To me, it is simply the agent of uniqueness in every person.

We see the folly of hoping for full self-understanding when we accept the fact that in every person there is an element of the unknown; a portion of personality that defies the limits of language and perception. The daimon is the unknown, and that is precisely why we fear it. Man is essentially a controller. Most of our lives we devote to mastering methods of control—over ourselves, over others, over our environment. When we are confronted by that which we cannot control, fear smashes into our guts. Hence, to accept the presence of the daimon in each person is to strum the strings of fear. Yet, to refuse to accept it is to mold a life-style on a phony base.

May puts it this way:

To be guided by your daimon requires a fundamental humility. Your own convictions will always have an element of blindness and self-distortion; the one ultimate illusion is to operate under the conceit that you are free from illusion. Indeed, some scholars believe the original Greek phrase "know thyself" means "Know that thou art only a man."[5]

I like that. I like it because it makes God's act of accepting me even bigger than my perception. God does know me—better than I know myself. He still accepts me —totally—for what I am. Knowing this, I need not understand myself beyond acknowledging that my vision is limited; I am only a man.

If, then, we are not intended to understand ourselves fully, what is our task? As far as I can perceive the challenge of Christ, it boils down to a question of responsibility. The important thing is not whether we understand ourselves or not, but our willingness to take responsibility for our actions—positive and negative.

Judas has long symbolized the scum of humanity. The role in history of Christ's betrayer epitomizes what everybody doesn't want to be. I disagree with that point of view. To me, Judas—for a brief period—showed more faith in Christ than any of the other disciples. I cannot admire his lust for money; I can respect his sense of humor. He had walked with the Lord for a long time. During the course of their relationship he had witnessed tremendous power in the Master: healing the lame, calming storms, raising the dead. In the light of those miracles, he reasoned, the threat posed by a handful of soldiers and a group of navel-gazing Pharisees was negligible. It was an easy thirty bucks for him and a much-needed lesson for them. So he "set up" the Lord. How was he to know that God had willed this to be the decisive event leading to the Crucifixion?

When, amazingly, the soldiers succeeded in taking his leader, Judas hated himself so much that he hanged himself. That's where he blew it. His faith was so weak that he couldn't perceive a risen Lord loving him in spite of his action. Judas should be despised not because he quit on Christ, but because he quit on himself! Horrified at what he had done, he placed his timetable ahead of Christ's. Unable to live with himself, he destroyed himself. What would have happened if Judas had taken responsibility for his act, gone to the Lord, and sought his forgiveness. Not in my wildest dreams can I imagine Jesus rejecting him. God did not will the death of Judas—Judas did.

What news this is for those of us who have spent painful hours in self-analyzation. We don't have to understand why we do what we do. What matters is our willingness to take responsibility for our persons, place ourselves in His grace, and practice the patience to wait for Him to grant our fulfillment according to His timetable.

To work with preachers week in and week out, as I do, is to truly stretch one's personality. It's one thing to believe you are called to a unique ministry, unlike that of anyone else. It's something else to get your balloon busted every week when you find someone with the same calling. You learn to pigeonhole your associates. A repeated phrase, a facial expression, a favorite style of humor—any of these is enough to box the other guy. The classic, for me, is the minister who goes to all the trouble of scheduling a program and then when the time comes just sits back and does nothing. Talk about instant indignation—that burns my nose every time.

We were once working in a church of about nine hundred members. There were two pastors on the staff. The associate minister was right with us, always available, obviously glad to get a chance to meet and be met. Not so the senior pastor. His gruff manner was matched only by an uncanny ability to disappear each night during the second (activities) phase of the program. I loved him, but I didn't like him. On the last night I was walking into the chancel when the associate stopped me.

"Hey, Barry," he said, "Ted and I want you to know how much this has meant to our church. We just hope we can keep it going."

I couldn't believe it. I said what I was thinking. "Well, if Ted thinks it's so beautiful, where in the heck has he been?"

"I can tell you now (he didn't want you to know earlier—thought it might hurt the program). He's going in for an operation tomorrow. They think he has a malignant tumor."

I shriveled at the recollection of my prejudice. There was no way I could start the service at that moment; responsibility beckoned. I found Ted closing the door of his study. At my apology, he gave me a warm smile and placed a hand on my shoulder. "Don't let me get in your way," he said.

He wasn't in my way—*I* was. I had chosen to believe that he didn't care about the program. In truth, he cared so much that he wouldn't let personal concerns interfere. My timetable had led to a hasty personal judgment that couldn't have been more wrong. God's timetable provided the grace to free me from my blindness. Once again God showed me that I do have illusions. Was I any nearer to knowing myself? No. But I was a lot closer to realizing that my ability to understand my behavior has nothing to do with the eternal presence of God's love. Humbled by what I am, I know that the hole in the ceiling answers my responsible actions with a peace that cannot be diminished.

In effect what this means is that there is a point beyond which searching the self is an exercise in futility. Complete self-knowledge is beyond our reach and irrelevant besides. Personal freedom does not come from knowing the self, it comes from knowing the One who—in spite of our weakness—accepts that self. I have known scores of people who wasted their lives asking "why" they did what they did while totally avoiding the consequences of their actions. Consider the fool who slashes his wrists and dies while contemplating his motive. Better to apply the tourniquet and *then* worry about the underlying cause. Again Keith Miller provides some insight: "There is a sense in which I reach a point at which I have looked at my situation until any more direct attention to it, even in prayer, becomes a step away from Christ. I have to walk away in raw faith believing that God will work beneath the scab."[6]

The key to peace lies in the courage to allow that frail,

divided, inconsistent, misunderstood self to be loved. That is a challenge. To believe that I am loved by another person is difficult for me; I know my feet stink. But to believe that I am loved by One who is all-perfect is frightening. It demands the confession of inadequacy and the acknowledgment of a power that exceeds my experience. It demands that I take responsibility for what I do, whether I understand my motives or not.

Part of this taking responsibility involves the ability to change course according to opportunity. My comfort is most secure when I know where I am going. For this reason I make it a habit to bargain with myself. I promise me that I will never do certain things again. Like the time I had a miserable experience conducting an outside celebration at a campground. The PA system failed, the guitarist didn't show, and midway through my talk a mosquito flew right in my mouth. As I drove away, I said to myself, "Johnson, if you ever say yes to one of these things again you're a dummy." That made me feel better. Three weeks later I broke the promise to myself and scheduled a whole summer series. Why? Because it involved growth-oriented people who didn't care if mosquitoes flew in my mouth. It was an opportunity. I believe God works that way. He lets us promise ourselves all kinds of things, but when he wants us to burst through the bondage of our promises, he throws us opportunities that can't be denied. In so doing he proves his sovereignty once again. Whereas our shortness of vision would seal off the future, his providence reveals new paths, new joy, and new hope. Our concept of self is encouraged when we recognize his hand at work in our lives.

Jonathan Livingston Seagull—as splendid an individual as has ever been conceived by a novelist—built a life-style by breaking self-imposed barriers: "His vows of a moment before were forgotten, swept away in that great swift wind. Yet he felt guiltless, breaking the promises he had made himself. Such promises are only for the gulls that accept the ordinary. One who has touched excellence in his learning has no need of that kind of promise."[7]

To limit oneself on the basis of personal experience is to deny the presence of a God who leads us out of the ordinary into a life-style filled with mountaintops. I may be so ignorant as to register displeasure over an experience. I hope I am never so pretentious as to assume that God can't make the darkest moment bright. The hole in the ceiling functions best when I recognize the limits of myself and cast my lot with the Self.

Consider the man caught in the tangle of a love affair. The more he seeks to understand "why," the deeper is his involvement. Hours of introspection limit his vision to what *he* wants, what *he* needs, and what *he* feels. He is trapped by himself. The daimon which makes him what he is prevents him from seeing beyond himself. Relief comes only when he vanquishes the self and reaches to those convictions which exist apart from the self. What is right, regardless of circumstance? What will bring growth as opposed to decay? And, finally, what is most responsible? The greatest service any therapist can perform for a marital difficulty is to provide a bridge between subjective illusions and objective facts. It's the best way I know to unmask the chimera of the self, force people to deal with reality, and underline the meaning of the grace of God.

Still another problem regarding a Christian perspective of the self extends beyond the limits of understanding and the urgency of responsible action. Even when we admit our ignorance and own up to our actions, we still need to let ourselves be loved. Too often, when we come hard against what we are, we quit. Sometimes, as in the

94

case of Judas, this means physical suicide. More frequently it means surrender to boredom, meaninglessness, and monotony—spiritual suicide. To live with the self is to let the self (good, bad, and ugly) be loved. I am ashamed of my occasional bad language, but I know I'm loved in spite of it and I don't quit on myself because of it.

In watching Bill Johnson work with released convicts I have seen the results of this theory both ways: those letting themselves be loved love in return; those refusing to be loved are incapable of giving love. Bill constantly amazes me with his perseverance in spite of circumstances. I have seen him work for weeks to get a man a job only to learn that the guy has stolen from his new employer and returned to jail. Do you think Bill quits? Never. He's right back at the jail talking with the guy, writing him letters, considering new job opportunities, loving the man in spite of his folly. Usually the result is a rearranged value system for the prisoner. But from time to time the exception will appear. The empty face, the shiftless attitude, and a resignation to failure are all there. These are the most disturbing cases to me. They are so down on themselves that they are incapable of responding to help.

This is the point where I grow impatient with the old evangelistic method based on fear. When we stress sinfulness, dwell on the torments of hell, and underscore the ugliness of man, we only reinforce our fallen state. By emphasizing our unacceptability we build walls that rebuff those who love us in spite of that unacceptability. Tillich's pronouncement "You are accepted" leaps over the weakness of man and wraps him in eternal love. He can't lose it. He can only refuse to accept it and in so doing cut himself off from the joy of being a whole person.

Helmut Thielicke put it this way: "If a person is steeped in emptiness and boredom and is tired of life, the reason for it is that he has not allowed himself to be loved by *God* and has not put himself in his hands. One who does not love makes the other person wither and dry up. And one who does not allow himself to be loved dries up too. For love is a creative thing."[8]

So look at yourself. If you're bored, empty, and tired of life, it would be wise to check your intake valves. Have you allowed yourself to be near people who love you? Have you learned that your failings are not all-consuming? Can you accept the fact that your mistakes and shortcomings cannot diminish the love of God? Are you willing to let your self mingle with other selves regardless of whether you understand your motivation or theirs?

Years ago Clinton Duffy came to be warden at San Quentin. Prior to his arrival that prison was noted for its ability to dehumanize. Riots were commonplace, and a general disregard for human life—both of inmates and staff—prevailed. Within six months the pattern was broken. It started the first day when, during a free exercise period, Clinton Duffy—without protection—casually strolled among the prisoners. It was an unheard of action; some said he would be dead within a week if he kept it up. He did. Not for a week, but for his entire term as warden. Clinton Duffy knew a very basic truth that is essential to a Christian view of the self: if you want to touch, you cannot fear being touched.

It is my conviction that God uses the self more than any other medium to express his constant love. Through the self he magnifies not only the wonder of man but the limits of man. Then, by accepting our extremes—good or bad—he reveals his character. And it still comes down to our perception. God is always there, waiting to affirm. Only when we learn to see beyond our weaknesses do we begin to sense the colossal nature of his love. The thrill comes from realizing that his power to love through, over, around, under, and in complete disregard of our ignorance is a channel of unending power for us. A distraught mother, shaken by the ramifications of this, once screamed in my face, "According to you, we can do ANYTHING!" Her concern evoked empathy in me. I knew what she was feeling. My response came after a moment of quiet that helped both of us relax: "Right, we can do ANYTHING. The difference is in the point of view. *I'm* talking about an infinite opportunity to grow. *You're* worried about moral license."

Years ago I set as one of my goals the systematic annihilation of any phony Christian process that limits man. Recently, I have been delighted to find that others share that goal. Never before has there been such an emphasis on wholeness, renewal, sanctification, and discipleship. After a century of overemphasis on man's failings, we have finally chosen to emphasize his potential. So long as that stress on the positive draws its strength from the sovereign will of God to make every self beautiful, we can anticipate increasing joy. By recognizing the unimportance of complete self-understanding, by pushing ourselves to take responsibility for our total persons, and by simply letting ourselves be loved, we shall become a true generation of hole-knockers.

Consider again *Jonathan Livingston Seagull.* If for no other reason, this little book is a masterpiece because it sounds the call for wholeness in every reader:

He spoke of very simple things—that it is right for a gull to fly, that freedom is the very nature of his being, that whatever stands against that freedom must be set aside, be it ritual or superstition or limitation in any form.

"Set aside," came a voice from the multitude, "even if it be the Law of the Flock?"

97

"The only true law is that which leads to freedom," Jonathan said. "There is no other."

"How do you expect us to fly as you fly?" came another voice. "You are special and gifted and divine, above other birds."

"Look at Fletcher! Lowell! Charles-Roland! Judy Lee! Are they also special and gifted and divine? No more than you are, no more than I am. The only difference, the very only one, is that they have begun to understand what they really are and have begun to practice it."[9]

In concluding this chapter I want to share a story that always leads to dynamic discussion. The story involves a promising preacher. While he was still in seminary, the word leaked out about Ralph Evans: this guy was a winner; preaching, administrating, and pastoring—he could do it all. Ultimately he found himself in a large church. It was his dream and he played his role perfectly. He was smooth. One evening he found a short paper written by his fourteen-year-old daughter, entitled "My Father." Reading it, he was forced to see his own facade. The last line was the clincher: "My dad may not be the greatest person in the world, but he is the greatest preacher."

Ralph Evans was stunned. He had given himself to his role so completely that even his own daughter couldn't see him as a person. Right there, he vowed to give up the game. No longer would he preach to entertain; no longer would he sacrifice his family just to keep two or three gripers happy. The change started the next Sunday. Ralph preached about tithing—something he had always wanted to do. As the people left they mumbled to one another, "Ralph had a bad Saturday night." The next Sunday he hit another heavy topic, "The Priesthood of All Believers." After five successive weeks his parishioners couldn't take any more. "The Letter" was sent to the bishop. Three months later Ralph Evans was moved—not up, but down. His new charge lasted only a year. By now he realized that many people prefer a suffering servant preacher who delights in the role of doormat. Exactly five years after reading his daughter's treatise, Ralph Evans was back in the boonies where he had started. Of course, the other ministers in his conference were really buzzing about his decline. The rumors grew progressively worse, to the point where the conference publicity director decided he had to get the true story from Evans himself.

"Ralph," the PR man said, "you had it made. Everybody envied you: big church, nice salary, two associates—the whole thing. What happened?"

The preacher made a man by a daughter's candor stared at the steam rising from his coffee cup. When he spoke, his words were deliberately clear: "It finally dawned on me that when I meet the Lord, he is not going to ask me, 'Why were you not Norman Vincent Peale? Why were you not Martin Luther King? Or why were you not Harry Emerson Fosdick?' No. All He's going to ask me is, 'Why were you not Ralph Evans?' "

In creating each of us as unique individuals God purposed that we be precisely who and what we are. Anything else is phony.

Chapter Nine

The Light in Love

The headline read "Faded Star Squints in Bright Lights." Beneath it newspaperman Tom Fitzpatrick pieced together a story about a fallen entertainer. From $10,000 per album and $2,500 a week she had slipped to a job singing in a neighborhood bar. Bad marriages, dope, and jail terms paved the downward path. Now, the patrons have stopped talking. Not for her. Her set is finished. She had to sing over the noise. It's the bass player who's captured attention. He's doing his thing, really into it, so wrapped up in the music that he can't feel her cold, hard, contemptuous stare. Finally, she walks to his side: physically, only three feet away; emotionally, a lifetime apart. He plays on for a moment before glancing at her expectantly. All he wants is a smile, a nod, maybe even a wink of encouragement. She yawns in his face; the ultimate putdown.

When I read that story it stunned me. It wasn't hard to remember the times when I have figuratively yawned in somebody's face. Also, I know the pain of receiving such a compliment. Unfortunately, when it happened to me it wasn't intentional. I wish it had been. I was in the midst of a message when a little kid sitting near the front dropped a yawn on me. It was devastating. I chose to believe that no one had noticed but me. It still sticks in my mind today. As you might guess, I've changed that message. The kid might have been up late the night before, or played baseball all afternoon, or even had a chronic yawning disease—it doesn't matter. The point is, his action rattled my battle plan.

In *Love and Will* Rollo May makes a simple yet pertinent statement that will help make my point. "Hate is not the opposite of love—apathy is!" The beauty of that insight is not wasted in Christian circles. How many times do we take pride in announcing, "I really don't hate anyone." Right; but we sure can be indifferent. It may sound silly, but I often feel that the Kingdom of God would prosper if we could muster a little hate; at least we'd have to take a stand. And when we care enough to take a stand it's easy to knock holes in the ceiling.

A few years ago talk-back sermons were revered as the "only honest way to preach." "After all," the argument went, "it's only fair to give the people their turn at bat." Sometimes it took a few months of courage-cranking, but most preachers ultimately gave "talk-backs" a try. The results were interesting. Topics, prevailing conditions, and questioning methods all played a role. Some churches were so excited by the method they made it a monthly practice. Others never knew it had happened in the first place. One New England pastor says the talk-back brought him closer to his people than anything in his ministry. Not because they liked it; they didn't. In fact, after four straight weeks he had found only a handful of people willing to stay for the discussion. Most didn't care either way. So he proceeded to write a sermon of blasphemy, including every major theological concern he could think of and refuting them all. When he walked into the fellowship hall after the service there wasn't an empty chair. Everybody had stayed. As he put it, "It was one of the finest open forums we have ever had. The people still talk about it."

The great challenge of being a Christian today is knowing how to love. Sometimes it can only be achieved by first determining what we don't love. I realize that this is a negative approach, but I also know we must meet people where they are. My work has taught me that people are much more able to discuss their hurts than their happiness. Once they have aired their dissatisfaction it is thoroughly emancipating to ask them about their joys. Of course, it is not unusual to see an empty face, gaping mouth, and troubled eyes at that point. That is the moment for creative concern. It is amazing what a few moments of positive insight can do for the hole in the ceiling. Like the bass player in Fitzpatrick's story, there are hundreds of people in our lives every week who are taking the risk of revealing their wants, dreams, and abilities. Ours is the choice: to encourage their efforts—or yawn in their face. Ours is the choice whether or not to love.

What we do is determined by the breadth of our vision. If we are free to see each person—regardless of dogma or deeds—as a child of God, we are free to love. However (and I fear that this is the case with too many neon Christians), if our vision is stunted by our own experiences, if we can only affirm those who affirm us, if we can only accept those who accept us, our love is perverted. It is not based on giving. It is based on receiving reflections of ourselves. This is my problem with dogmatic Christians of both the liberal and the conservative stripe. Both claim love as the basis of their actions, yet remain totally indifferent to the success or failure of those who differ with them. To love in such a way that the presence of God is illuminated by one's actions is to care—positively or negatively.

My experience has been that the most adept "people-lovers" are those who admit to a missing link in their faith. Devoid of the holy arrogance that forbids displays of weakness, these folk have the capacity to cry, laugh, guess, and doubt publicly. They come on very real as a result. When they care about you, they show it. Rather than plastic smiles, they give quiet, comtemplative attention. It is as though their own joy is not nearly as important as mine. They don't protect themselves with bubbly facades and self-demeaning platitudes. On the contrary, they seem to want to get involved regardless of vulnerability.

Risk, then, becomes a distinguishing mark of Christian love. Bill Taegel makes an eloquent case for such openness as he describes "if-love," "because-love," and "anyhow-love."[10] The first depends on what others can do for us. If you dress like me . . . if you witness like me . . . if you share my sense of humor . . . if you meet my needs—I will love you. There's no risk in that process; it's just a matter of getting the right reflection.

"Because-love" is just a little better. But again, it is a love predicated upon the other person's actions. Because you fed me when I was hungry . . . because you watched my kids while I went shopping . . . because you paid my way to the bullfight—I will love you. By basing love on what the other person does, security is still maintained and the lover is free from responsibility for his action. There is no risk. Like the third domino in the toppled row, there is no way he can be blamed for the actions of number one.

The final form, "anyhow-love," demands the greatest risk because it depends on independent decisions by the lover, not on the actions of the other person or ulterior motives. Put simply, it boils down to a choice between risking or not risking. "Anyhow-love" pays no heed to what the other person is willing to return or has already done; it's just there. All it requires is a decision to get involved without concern for consequences. It exemplifies what Christ did for all of us. The hole in my ceiling reaches infinite proportions when I realize that, regardless of what I do, God loves me ANYHOW!

What this means to me is that I have no license to demand that others reflect my position before I give them my love. Whether another person worships Jesus Christ or Abbie Hoffman, whether he drinks Kool-Aid or guzzles Bloody Marys, whether he lives with his wife or the town whore—as a follower of Christ, I am called to love him.

So what is the motivation of the Christian witness? To win souls for Christ? No way. That is manipulation. It is loving others *because* rather than *anyhow*. The motivation of the Christian witness is to let Christ's love live through him—period. Winning souls is the task of the Holy Spirit, and the best thing I can do to help is to love—*anyhow*.

As I mentioned earlier, I have always felt awkward among glowing, ever-happy Christians. Most often it was because I wasn't in their league. Witnessing and ringing up conversions just wasn't my bag. Then I took the time to ask myself who had made the greatest witness to me. Of the four people who came to mind, only one had ever *witnessed* in the traditional sense in my presence. The others were people who had consistently loved me *anyhow*.

That is the basic difference between authentic and plastic witnessing for Christ. Those who are honestly concerned about the wholeness made possible in Christ will give complete attention to helping other persons to affirm themselves as children of God and be what he wants them to be. The plastic witnesser, on the other hand, seeks only to create a carbon copy of himself. This was the disservice performed by early missionaries. On the assumption that being saved meant praying, dressing, marrying, and living just like they did, they literally destroyed the cultures they encountered. Fortunately, such practices have changed as we have come to understand that the love of Christ includes both bare-breasted African tribeswomen and prim Philadelphia grandmothers. To love somebody in Christ's name is to love them the way they are.

The Greek philosophers distinguished various forms of love, of which I want to single out three for discussion. Perhaps you are already familiar with them, but I still want to call attention to them, not so much for the sake of intellectual definition as to indicate the elusive and complex nature of love itself.

The first is *phileo*. This is the kind of love shared by good friends. Mutually enabling, it depends on such things as compatibility and communication. David and Jonathan enjoyed this kind of love (see 1 Samuel 18). The depth of their commitment is highlighted by Jonathan's willingness to warn David when Saul sought to kill him. By so opposing the will of his own father, Jonathan indicated that *phileo* can be as fervent as any other form of love.

Eros, the second form, is probably the most misunderstood of all the forms of love. If you are like me, as soon as you hear that word you think of sexual escapades, real and imagined. The Greek word does indeed mean sexual love, but that is not the only area of life where *eros* functions. In a wider sense it is present wherever love is self-serving. To that extent those who love to witness for Christ because they are thrilled by leading people to him are nursing an erotic urge. Think about that. Wouldn't it be a kick to casually inform Joe Wonderful Witnesser that his eroticism is out of hand? You might get erroneously branded a sex-maniac, but it sure would throw light on his motivation.

The motion-picture *Patton* contains a classic example of *eros*. The scene is a battlefield just a few hours after the clash. Smoke is rising from battered tanks, the ground is littered with dead and wounded, and cries of anguish can still be heard. In the midst of all that, Patton smacks his fist in his palm and, with blazing eyes, exclaims, "I love it. I love it." He loved war because war served his purposes; only in war could his genius be satisfied. His love was based on fulfilling himself. *Eros* is always like that. The object of such love is secondary to the desire to satisfy self-need. In that light a self-satisfied witnesser is even more disturbing. The fact that he witnesses to you doesn't mean a thing about what he thinks of you; it only means *he* has the need to witness for his own sake.

Agape is the form of love most often linked with Christ. This is love that sacrifices self for the continuing relationship. And that brings me to what could be a volatile point: the continuing relationship is the issue. Christ knew that eternity was his. For him, to die was but to experience a new, fuller life-style. His sacrifice was the bridge between temporal and eternal love. When he laid down his life, he did it for the sake of an infinitely continuing relationship with humanity. I am not sure that any other man can make such a claim. This is not to say that there have been no sincere martyrs who died for others. But Jesus Christ is the only man who ever died to fulfill a relationship.

Of course, *agape* can exist in less extreme situations than that of life and death. While serving in Bensenville I met a teen-ager who made a consistent practice of *agape*. Whenever someone had to relinquish a seat for an adult, Bobby did it. Whenever special work groups were formed, Bobby volunteered. And whenever someone had to be left behind for lack of car space, Bobby stayed home. It would have been different if the kid had been a namby-pamby. Not Bobby. He was a big, solid guy who seemed to understand that when he put himself second, other people put him first. It wasn't a matter of life or death, but it was still *agape*. He gave of himself for the sake of others.

So there they are, three forms of love: *phileo, eros,* and *agape*. Each has identifying characteristics, but lest we become too conscious of labels, I want to make one more very important observation about the forms of love. Never have I found any of these forms existing in isolation. Always, regardless of circumstance, they are interwoven. Consider the examples I have used. Patton loved war because it fulfilled his need; but he also gave his life to the study of the thing he loved. Jonathan was so committed to his friend that he warned him of danger; but he was also reasonably assured that sometime David would return the favor. Still, he risked himself for his friend. Bobby made it a practice to sacrifice his own wishes for the sake of the group, but in so doing he was well aware that they would love him in return; he was also committed to friendship. And finally, even Jesus Christ didn't practice *agape* in isolation. The sacrifice was there, but so was a lifetime of friendly relationships and the knowledge that his action would be pleasing to his Father and thereby beneficial to himself.

The hole in the ceiling finds new glory when we realize that none of us are called upon to practice perfect love, any more than Christ did. As human beings who place value on friendships, personal gain, and the ability to sacrifice, we are expected to love in the fullest sense, using all the forms, all the time, all together.

And whatever we do, let's avoid the trap of making a head-game of our loving. Picture a moonlit lagoon on a cool summer evening. A car pulls up to the edge of the water, turns off its lights, and parks. Forty-five minutes later the windows are fogged and the occupants in a state of emotional upheaval. The young man speaks: "Darling, I love you!"

Can you imagine her answering, "What do you mean, honey—*eros, phileo,* or *agape?*"

Of course not! Why is it then that we spend so much time measuring the motivations of love? By concentrating on what makes things happen, we postpone their occurrence. By asking why my wife loves me I create a pseudo-intellectual filter through which she has to work to love me. The issue becomes so complicated that love—which has a spontaneous nature anyhow—is rendered powerless. I for one refuse to worry about *why* my wife loves me. Knowing my shortcomings the way I do, I am thrilled that she loves me at all. Who cares *why?*

Carry that line of thought to man's relationship with Christ. No matter how long we think about it, the chances of ever convincing ourselves that we are worthy of Christ's love are extremely slim. Those caught up with earning God's love face a similar problem. They can never do enough to be comfortable as recipients. The whole Christian recognizes that the omnipotence of God's love far exceeds anything he may or may not do. In the most simple terms, what man does means nothing. God's decision to love has already been made affirmatively. Just as my relationship with my wife suffers if I seek to intellectualize it, so does my relationship with Christ. I either accept his offer to be there for me, or I refuse to recognize it. My self is either whole in him or fragmented alone. And, never can I be so ignorant as to imagine that

108

what I say or do can influence the power of God's love. Were that true, his love would be subject to my whims and fancies. Such a love would certainly not endure for eternity. And when all other measures of God's love fall by the wayside, its ability to touch the boundaries of eternity will be the deciding issue. A love that originates beyond the limits of man's experience will continually transcend those limits. The hole in the ceiling blinds me with light when I accept the infinity of God's love; and life and death become less overwhelming.

I am going to close this chapter with a letter. It comes from Robert Raines' *Soundings*. Since I have two small children who brighten my life, I find it especially moving. It is a letter that shows us that the love of God is the greatest hole-knocker we can ever know, even in the face of disaster.

Dear Friends:

Our Stevie was a special gift from God to us. He was given a good, strong body, a fine and inquisitive mind, and a warm and sensitive heart for people and for animals. His last task from his hospital bed was finding a good family for each one of his six curly black-haired puppies.

We were so proud of our gallant little fellow who fought so bravely. "Please read to me, Mommie, from my Bible of the miracles which Jesus did," he used to say, "You know, Daddy, when it hurts so much and I become afraid, I pray and ask God for courage and he always helps me get through."

The time was short. His Daddy took him on Thursday, September 12, to the hospital. He had one completely collapsed lung. For ten days, the lung specialist tried to restore the lung to activity, but was hindered by a tumor which gave reason for suspicion. An exploratory operation of the abdomen confirmed that our Stevie suffered from a very malignant, fast-growing cancer which had invaded his whole system. On Saturday morning, September 28, both of us, in a circle of love and prayers, accompanied our son to the entrance of this other existence, where pain and sadness have lost their power.

On Sunday morning early, Richard discovered in our yard a beauti-

ful orchid blossom. We had brought those plants from Hawaii, but the California climate was not suitable for them. So many times Richard had admonished Stevie to water them more often, but they seemed so sad and dry to us that we had given up hope on them—and then appeared this beautiful blossom on the day of Stevie's departure and a second one on the day of his burial. It was to us like Stevie's laughter, saying to us in his witty way, "Dad, the joke is on you. Life has more power than death."

The Memorial Service was held in the Chapel of Friendship at the Spanish American Institute. Rev. Melvin Talbert, our Superintendent, directed our eyes to the life everlasting and when he asked, "Will we see our loved one again?" Markus, who is very lonely for Stevie, nodded his head vigorously in affirmation. A friend sang a part from "Amahl and the Night Visitors" which Stevie loved to sing with his good, clear voice. Hymns of faith resounded in the Chapel and something wonderful, like the joy and victory of Easter morning, entered our hearts. Yes, our God can give songs in the night.

We buried our son on a lovely hillside at the Green Hills Memorial Park in San Pedro. His Dad, who had consecrated him at the altar as a baby and baptized him when he asked for it as a six-year-old, committed his body to the earth. There on the lofty hillside, Heidi and Markie and we, his parents, sang him his beloved round, "The Lord's My Shepherd, I walk with him always."

Richard and Lean Acosta
with Heidi and Markie[11]

Chapter Ten

The Light in the Word

In the preceding nine chapters I have tried to show how one can be aware of the presence of God anytime, any the time, once one understands that the Word of God is any medium that communicates his love for mankind. By concentrating on man, circumstance, hope, freedom, forgiveness, growth, community, selfhood, and love, I have placed before you the many parts of what I consider to be a whole attitude. The following three incidents serve as proof that we can sense God's guidance in every situation. Furthermore, they testify to a Word of God that is bigger than the Bible, a Word that comes from life itself.

Ed's Garage

The garage is located on the main thoroughfare in a little blue-collar town. Out in front there may be as many as twenty used cars, though rarely any that cost more than two thousand dollars. Ed Schmitz makes a living off the secondhand car market, helped by an easygoing manner and a wealth of mechanical talent. In effect, it's a one-man operation, but you'd never know it by looking. Always there are two or three characters standing around putting forth the best down-home philosophy within a hundred miles of Chicago. In the eight years that I have frequented the garage there has always been one lead philosopher. Periodically the chair changes hands, but it's always filled. While still in school I discovered how refreshing it was to shift worlds by spending an occasional afternoon sitting on an oil drum in Ed's Garage. Now, when I need a break from business, I can always find a hole in the ceiling at Ed's.

Today, there are only two men there besides Ed, who is under a '71 Ambassador trying to fix an axle bearing. Jim Bridges presently holds the chair of lead philosopher. In addition, a gentleman in blue coveralls with "George" embroidered on the left side of the chest is leaning against the wall griping about the grain monopoly in the United States.

As I come through the door Bridges spots me and ventures the traditional greeting: "Will you look at this, Ed—the preacher's back. Where the heck you been?"

Two years ago Ed lost the use of his left ear. If you don't catch him right, he can't understand what you say. From under the car comes his most frequent response. "Uh?"

"I said the preacher's here. Come to reclaim this lousy car." Bridges is nearly leaning under the Ambassador.

Now I recognize the car. I had prevailed upon Ed to take a friend of mine to the used car auction and let him choose his own car. The friend chose the Ambassador, then changed his mind and took a Chevrolet that Ed had bought the same day. That left Ed with an Ambassador that he never would have bought for himself. Fortunately, an American Motors fan came along and bought the car, but the episode was still a sore point.

"I'm going back outside till you guys finish this conversation," I say.

My remark evokes tri-part laughter that tells me two things. First, the point wasn't really that sore. Second, it was sore enough for George to know all about the deal.

I sit down by the coffeepot—it's actually a mud caldron—and the lead philosopher starts to muse about Watergate. Bridges isn't exactly sympathetic to any Republican cause, so he scorches Nixon pretty good. George just nods approval, and Ed keeps on working—he's heard this one before. After a few topic changes, Bridges notices that I'm taking notes. "What the hell are you, preacher—some kind of inspector?"

"Right! I want all new wiring in this firetrap by next week."

I must have caught Ed on the right side, as the next voice issues from under the car. "I'll sell it first!"

"Really, Ed, he's writin' stuff down in some notebook."

Bridges is a little nervous about being recorded, so I tell him that I'm writing a book. I shouldn't have. For the next three hours he makes it a point to share deeper insights.

Ed scooches out from under the car with a damaged seal in his hand. "Watcha been doin'?" He speaks louder than necessary just to show his warmth. We're good friends and we understand each other. Ed's son, Keith, was in my catechism class while I was a student assistant at their church. The kid is a good athlete, and Ed and I have traveled miles together to watch him compete. Betty, Ed's wife, is a beautiful lady with an unforgettable personality and a heart of gold. Over eight years we have developed a solid friendship. I hope it lasts forever.

"Runnin' and writing . . . trying to stay out of jail," I say in answer to Ed's question.

"Keith's ready to quit working and go out for football. He sure hates that factory."

"Best thing that ever happened to him."

"You better believe it—bet it shows in his grades next semester, too."

Ed makes a phone call and sends me and Bridges to pick up a new axle seal. The rest of the afternoon is spent watching the Cubs lose to Atlanta 6–2, talking with Bridges about his racehorses, and resisting a sales pitch about a used Grand Prix. We part with me telling Ed that Celeste will call Betty about getting together for a barbecue before Keith goes back to school.

As I pull out of the driveway, I realize that the hole in the ceiling at Ed's Garage is just a matter of acceptance with no strings attached, and I vow that, this year, I'll get there more often.

Flight 869

It was to be a one-day venture, and by leaving my car in the parking garage at O'Hare I would save Celeste the trouble of picking me up. At 6:00 A.M. the radio came on and I got up. Dane was in our bed, and when the noise of my fiddling around woke her Tracy joined him. As I walked down the hall I let our dog, Cus, out of the den. The last sound I heard as I left the house was the screams of delight as he joined the group.

Departure time was 7:10. The plane left on time. I didn't. Even though I ran like a fool all the way to gate E-10 (next to farthest from the terminal), the plane was rolling away as I reached the desk. The clerk laughed and punched the counter-top computer. He booked me on the next flight at 8:40. Secretly I had wanted to eat breakfast at the airport anyhow.

At 8:10 we were allowed to board. A young couple ambled down the ramp in front of me. He was tall, solidly built, and obviously trying to be brave. I reacted negatively to his crew cut. She was thin, quite pretty, and the reason he was trying to be brave. Ironically, their seats

114

were adjacent to mine. The takeoff was smooth, but their comments gave them away as first-flighters.

"Wow, that's pressure."

"My ears are popping."

"Look at the size of those cars."

I was getting into a paperback when the voice of a stewardess broke my concentration. "Would you like one roll or two?"

"One, thanks."

A second stewardess was coming down the aisle with a tray of coffee. As she reached my seat, we hit turbulence. The first few bumps were harmless and she displayed her training by deftly balancing the tray, not spilling a drop. The third bump blew the whole show. The coffee went up, the tray went down, and I found myself with eight cups of coffee in my lap. One cup flew across the big guy's lap and zapped his wife. Her pastel pantsuit didn't handle the problem as well as my black slacks. I really felt sorry for her. Apparently my face mirrored my feelings, and her husband responded to my sympathy.

"You fly much?" he inquired.

His smile was warm, and I regretted my hasty interpretation of his crew cut. "Yes, a bunch," I replied.

"This is the first time for my wife. How much of this bouncing do we need to anticipate?"

"Not much. They usually get above it."

"You in business for yourself? Oh, I'm sorry, I don't mean to be nosy—just friendly."

"That's OK. Yes, I am."

"What do you do?"

"Church renewal work. Things like leadership development and motivation."

"What denomination?"

"All of 'em. We specialize in putting them together."

His wife touched his leg and he turned back to her. "He reminds me of Darrell Swaringen," she said.

Both of them spoke with a touch of a drawl. "Where you from?" I asked.

"Decatur, Illinois. We're off to look at a new job possibility."

I knew I recognized that drawl: my hometown is just north of Decatur. After that we started to talk about the new job. It was a joy to see their excitement about the future. He talked about contacting other men at the new plant and getting their impressions about the administration and the town. Their greatest concern was relocating two children (five and ten years old). I told them about our family's frequent moves over the last four years. That seemed to reassure the wife.

"Tell her about landing so she'll calm down," the husband instructed me.

"It's nothing," I said. "When they blow it, nobody even knows what hit 'em."

Panic showed in her eyes, and I knew I shouldn't have said that.

"No, really," I went on hurriedly, "there will be a little bounce as we touch down, then the engines will roar and you'll be able to see the sleeves open to brake our speed. I really think it's kind of fun."

"See, I told ya." He was being brave again.

The stewardess brought a wet cloth to clean up the coffee as the seat belt sign flickered on. We were in our final approach. Whether the pilot knew it or not, his soft landing saved me an explanation. I wished them luck with the new job and we shook hands and parted.

By sharing the hopes of others I had found a new hole in the ceiling. Such routine things as the thrill of leaving the ground and the security of touching it again made me thankful. I could laugh at a missed departure because God had helped me grow through a new one. And, most joyous of all, I found a new opportunity to share my Christian life-style, counting on him to make the experience a medium for his message.

The Ya-Ha Principle

I didn't want to go. It was the end of the summer, and we were experiencing a slack in scheduling. A new advertising project was under way, and I wanted to keep my finger on it. Besides that, the retreat was to be held at Honey Rock Camp (owned by Wheaton College) near Eagle River, Wisconsin. Returning to the atmosphere of the college didn't excite me at all. Celeste assured me that it wouldn't be a "Wheaton thing," because Chuck Gieser of Christ Church, Oakbrook, was running it. He is a Wheaton grad, but he has a style all his own. Even so, it was with great reservations that I bid the office adieu for the week. Had I known what was before me I would have left a day early.

Fourteen families gathered at the campground, where the only obvious mark of Wheaton was the cream-colored paint on the buildings (popular in the college maintenance department) and a common commitment to Jesus Christ. Each day reinforced my opinion that Chuck Gieser is a super local church pastor. The idea of a family camp with baby-sitters provided and special family-oriented experiences all day every day is an indication of his sensitivity to a whole ministry. As the associate pastor at Christ Church he has added a much-needed dose of people-concern and evangelical depth to what could have been another sterile ecclesiastical mammoth*.

*Author's note: Chuck Gieser is now the executive director at Sky Ranch near Dallas, Texas.

I had made up my mind to keep my mouth shut during the evening sessions for parents, even though we were dealing with the Holy Spirit—my favorite theological topic. My plan worked for one night. During the second session someone asked if the Holy Spirit ever withholds counsel. Chuck responded with an analogy that popped my cork. Referring to his own relationship with his daughter, he explained that her disobedience often results in his refusal to comply with her requests. The inference was that our faults can cause God to withhold his guidance. I couldn't hack that. No way can I picture God being so petty as to hold a grudge. For me, the Holy Spirit is totally consistent. He never withholds counsel if we seek it, regardless of our disobedience. God is love. He consistently cares and communicates. Where we run into problems is in the psychological ramifications of our disobedience. Because we are aware of our failures, we tend to dwell on them too much. This results in introspective blindness. Trapped by concern for ourselves, we are insensitive to God's ever-present concern through the Holy Spirit. Never, regardless of what we do, does God refuse counsel.

I explained my position.

"Does that mean we can do anything and still come back to God?" one of the men asked.

"Yes."

"Then what is the unpardonable sin?"

I was caught. The Bible clearly states that blasphemy against the Holy Spirit is unpardonable. This has always been a problem for me. If there is a way to cut off God's love forever through a single act, that love can't be too powerful. My mind was churning for an answer when Rich Wagner, a public relations man from Hinsdale, clarified the issue. I had noticed Rich's familiarity with the Scriptures and sensed the presence of a fellow searcher. I listened carefully as he spoke. His insights threw fresh light on my growing faith. A new hole in the ceiling appeared.

"As I see it," Rich said, "the key issue in the Christian faith is forgiveness. It's a once-for-all thing. This means that God never withholds his love. It doesn't mean that we can't look the other way. The unpardonable sin is realizing the consistency of God's love and saying, *"Ya-ha!* I can do anything because he won't stop loving me!" In other words, willfully taking advantage of God! It's a matter of a ya-ha attitude as opposed to one of eternal thankfulness."

The whole group was doubled over with laughter at Rich's inflection on "Ya-ha." Chuck and I looked at each other and smiled; spiritual growth provides a common bond.

One more time the love of God had penetrated my life in an unexpected way through an encounter that I had almost missed. Through a sincere Christian layman I had found a solid answer to a long-standing personal dilemma. That night, after everyone was in bed, I slipped out into a clearing behind our cottage. As I gazed upward it seemed as though an endless multitude of stars twinkled above me. I thanked God for a new hole in the ceiling.

The Word of God is any medium that communicates the fact that God loves you—who you are, where you are, as you are. That means that all of us have an unending source of holes in the ceiling.

Appendix

Small Group Discussion Questions

Introduction: **The Search**
1. When was the last time you questioned the existence of God?
2. What are some of the methods you have used to draw nearer to God?
3. Is it possible to be over-confident about God's presence and love?
4. Have you ever felt your Christian friends were so busy being spiritual that they were insensitive to your needs? How do we avoid this?

Chapter One: **The Light in Man**
1. Is there a parallel to preaching the Good News? Action? Which comes first?
2. Have you ever sensed God's presence in another person? Explain.
3. Share an incident when the actions of a child made you sense God's love.
4. Do you have a Sancho Panza? Explain.
5. Think of each of the members of your family—does God speak to you through them? How?

Chapter Two: **The Light in Circumstance**
1. Have you ever had a close shave? Describe it.
2. Can you recall a time when your own attempt to control a situation backfired?
3. Have you ever taken a "leap of faith"?
4. What happened to you yesterday? Did God speak through any particular circumstance?

Chapter Three: **The Light in Hope**
1. Try to arrive at a common definition of *hope.*
2. What does the *Resurrection* mean to you?
3. Discuss the author's observation:
   When faced by sure defeat, we stop worrying about victory and start caring about dignity.
   When faced by death, we release our grip on the temporal and take note of the eternal.
   When faced by loss, we smother our greed and celebrate what we still have.
4. Was Jesus Christ a winner or a loser? Why?

Chapter Four: **The Light in Freedom**
1. What do you think "fear God" means?
2. Do you agree that a Christian is free to do anything?
3. Have you ever done anything like stealing the truck? Describe.
4. Can you recall any time when impulsiveness cost you dear?
5. Does freedom frighten you or make you uneasy?
6. Can you think of a personal acquaintance who practices love without concern for returns? Example?

Chapter Five: **The Light in Forgiveness**
1. Have you ever felt it impossible to forgive someone? If you wish, talk about the situation.
2. "True forgiveness never includes a contract." Discuss.
3. Did God love Richard Speck (convicted killer of eight student nurses in Chicago) when Speck was taking the lives of his victims?
4. Is there any offense that is unforgivable?
5. Can you think of any incident in your life where forgiveness was used to gain power? Explain.

Chapter Six: **The Light in Growth**
1. What limits are you aware of in your spiritual life? Rules, practices, expectations?
2. Has your (*a*) time commitment, (*b*) people-contact commitment, (*c*) financial commitment to Jesus Christ changed in the last year? If not, why not?
3. Is your faith best defined as a "position to be defended" or a "process to be lived"?

4. What have you done in the last year to keep your faith moving?
5. Choose a color to describe your prayer life. Explain.
6. Examine your life and the program of your church; in light of both what are you doing to "feed Christ's sheep"?

Chapter Seven: **The Light in Community**
1. Make a list of three piccolo-persons you intend to affirm within the next twenty-four hours. Discuss how.
2. Rank the following according to importance in your church: ____property ____program ____persons. · What can you do to make persons remain or become the first priority?
3. What is your personal opinion about the purpose of your worship services as they are now conducted?
4. Is there an obvious intent for each gathering?
5. Identify the various special characters in your congregation. Is anything being done to encourage individuality?
6. Is your church a sensitive church? Why? Why not?

Chapter Eight: **The Light in Selfhood**
1. Is there anything about yourself that you can't seem to understand or control? Explain.
2. Reread the paragraph dealing with the *daimon.* What is your most distinctive characteristic?
3. Do you know anyone who refuses to accept himself—who, what, and where he is?
4. What is your response to the illustration about Judas?
5. What are some of the ways that you shut yourself off from Christ's grace? Moodiness, sulking, busyness, worry?
6. Discuss the quote from Helmut Thielicke. Can you think of an incident in your life where love was creative like this?
7. Does your practice of Christianity magnify or reduce your unique personhood? How?

Chapter Nine: **The Light in Love**
1. Consider the world situation right now. Can you think of any areas where Christians are insensitive to need? What about in your own community?
2. Discuss the three kinds of love: "if-love," "because-love," and "anyhow-love." Which do you practice most often?

3. How do you respond to the idea that winning souls for Christ is erotic?
4. After reading the Acosta letter share any similar situations with which you are familiar.
5. Analyze some of your own love-relationships in terms of *phileo, eros* and *agape*.

Chapter Ten: **The Light in the Word**
1. Respond to the idea "The Word of God is any medium that communicates God's love for mankind." Do you agree? What does this mean for the authority of the Bible?
2. Do you have a place like Ed's Garage where you can change the pace of your life? Explain.
3. Can you remember a time (Flight 869) when you sensed God working in your relationship to someone else? Do you think God uses life-style witness as well as verbal witness?
4. When was the last time you did not want to do something (the Ya Ha Principle), did it anyway, and received a great blessing?

GOOD KNOCKING!

Notes

1. William C. Schutz, *Joy; Expanding Human Awareness* (New York: Grove Press, 1967), p. 9.
2. Jürgen Moltmann, *Theology of Hope* (New York: Harper & Row, 1967), p. 283.
3. Emil Brunner, *The Divine Imperative* (Philadelphia: The Westminster Press, 1947), p. 190.
4. James V. McConnell, "How to Take Control of Your Life," *Success Unlimited,* March 1973, p. 29.
5. Rollo May, *Love And Will* (New York: W. W. Norton & Co., 1969), p. 157.
6. Keith Miller, *A Second Touch,* (Waco, Tex.: Word Books, 1967), p. 77.
7. Richard Bach, *Jonathan Livingston Seagull* (New York: Avon Books, 1973), p. 27.
8. Helmut Thielicke, *How The World Began* (Philadelphia: Fortress Press, 1961), p. 180.
9. Bach, *Jonathan Livingston Seagull*, p. 114.
10. William S. Taegel, *People Lovers* (Waco Tex.: Word Books, 1972), pp. 18-19.
11. Robert Raines, *Soundings* (New York: Harper & Row, 1970), p. 68.